The Cambridge Introduction to
Toni Morrison

Toni Morrison has written some of the most significant and demanding
fiction of the modern age. Her dazzling depictions of African-American
experience are studied in high schools and colleges, debated in
the media, and analyzed by scholars at an astounding rate. This
Introduction offers readers a guide to the world of Morrison in all its
complexity, from her status as a key player on the global intellectual
stage to her unique perspective on American history and her innovative
narrative techniques. Covering every novel from *The Bluest Eye* to *A
Mercy*, Tessa Roynon combines close readings with critical insights into
Morrison's other creative work, such as short stories, libretto and song
lyrics, and unpublished pieces for performance. Chapters also highlight
the significance of Morrison's nonfiction, including her groundbreaking
work of literary criticism, *Playing in the Dark*, as well as her many
essays, speeches, and interviews. Lively and accessibly written, Roynon's
insightful text is ideal for readers approaching Morrison for the first
time as well as those familiar with her work.

Tessa Roynon teaches American literature at the University of Oxford.
Author of *Toni Morrison and the Classical Tradition: Transforming
American Culture* (2013) and co-editor of *African Athena: New Agendas*
(2011), she has published articles on Morrison widely, including in the
Journal of American Studies and *African American Review*.

The Cambridge Introduction to
Toni Morrison

TESSA ROYNON

CAMBRIDGE UNIVERSITY PRESS
Cambridge, New York, Melbourne, Madrid, Cape Town,
Singapore, São Paulo, Delhi, Mexico City

Cambridge University Press
32 Avenue of the Americas, New York, NY 10013-2473, USA

www.cambridge.org
Information on this title: www.cambridge.org/9780521177221

First published 2013

Printed in the United States of America

A catalog record for this publication is available from the British Library.

Library of Congress Cataloging in Publication data
Roynon, Tessa.
    The Cambridge introduction to Toni Morrison / Tessa Roynon.
        p.   cm. – (Cambridge introductions to literature)
    Includes bibliographical references and index.
    ISBN 978-1-107-00391-0 (hardback) – ISBN 978-0-521-17722-1 (pbk.)
    1. Morrison, Toni – Criticism and interpretation.   I. Title.   II. Title: Toni Morrison.
    PS3563.O8749Z8448   2012
    813'.54–dc23   2012029774

ISBN 978-1-107-00391-0 Hardback
ISBN 978-0-521-17722-1 Paperback

For my parents, Gavin and Patsy Roynon, with grateful love

Contents

Preface

In July 2008 I went to Charleston, South Carolina, for the conference of the Toni Morrison Society. The driver of my taxi from the airport erupted in enthusiasm when she heard where I was going. When she found out the program was to include Morrison reading from her not-yet-published novel *A Mercy*, she told me she would find a way to be in that theater herself. It is to state the obvious to say that not every Nobel Prize–winning author of complex, difficult novels, not every university professor who has produced critical work of broad and enduring intellectual significance, is held in this kind of esteem. There is something different about Toni Morrison.

Author of ten novels to date, Morrison has been translated into twenty-six languages. She has been a *Newsweek* cover; she is an institution on "Oprah's Book Club"; and she has honorary doctorates from the universities of Oxford and the Sorbonne. Her unique, challenging, and passionately political depictions of African-American experience are studied in high schools and colleges, discussed by reading groups and debated in all media, and published on by scholars at an astounding rate.

So much material and so much hype mean that to approach the world of Morrison for the first time is a little overwhelming. The aim of this book is to provide one way into and one path through that world. You will find here an overview of her life story, which emphasizes the experiences that have shaped her intellectually and politically. You will find detailed introductions to the first nine novels (*Home*, published in May 2012, postdates the submission of this manuscript), as well as consideration of her other creative work and nonfiction. There follows a discussion of the main contexts within which Morrison's oeuvre operates: African-American history and tradition, dominant American culture, African traditions, and transnational culture. The fourth and final chapter addresses the reception of Morrison's work: an overview of the critical field is followed by a brief discussion of her evolving status and reputation as a cultural icon. A Guide to Further Reading is at the end.

It is a great privilege to write this book, but it is also a responsibility. Morrison is a writer of such sophistication and moral seriousness that to distill the richness of her work into an introductory overview is no small challenge. The scholars, teachers, students, friends, and family who have contributed to my journey this far are too numerous to name individually, but I am indebted to all of them. To those of you just setting out on a study of this demanding but rewarding author, meanwhile, my advice repeats the words with which Florens begins the story of her journey in *A Mercy*: "Don't be afraid."

Abbreviations

Quotations will be cited in parentheses in the text by page number.

AM	*A Mercy* (2008) New York: Vintage, 2009.
B	*Beloved* (1987) New York: Vintage, 2005.
BB	*The Black Book.* Ed. Middleton Harris et al. (1974). 35th Anniversary Edition. New York: Random House, 2009.
BE	*The Bluest Eye* (1970) New York: Vintage, 1999.
BoN	*Birth of a Nation'hood: Gaze, Script, and Spectacle in the O. J. Simpson Case.* With Claudia Brodsky Lacour. New York: Pantheon, 1993.
BTB	*Burn This Book: PEN Writers Speak Out on the Power of the Word.* New York: Harper, 2009.
CL	"City Limits, Village Values: Concepts of the Neighborhood in Black Fiction." *Literature and the American Urban Experience: Essays on the City and Literature.* Ed. Michael C. Jayne and Ann Chalmers Watts. Manchester: Manchester University Press, 1981. 35–44.
DC	*Toni Morrison: Conversations.* Ed. Carolyn Denard. Jackson: University Press of Mississippi, 2008.
GiA	"Ghosts in the Attic." Hilton Als. *New Yorker* 27 Oct. 2003: 62–75.
H	"Home." *The House That Race Built: Black Americans, US Terrain.* Ed. Wahneema Lubiano. New York: Pantheon, 1997, 3–12.
J	*Jazz* (1992) New York: Vintage, 2005.
L	*Love* (2003) New York: Vintage, 2005.
NL	*Lecture and Speech of Acceptance, Upon the Award of the Nobel Prize for Literature, 1993.* New York: Knopf, 1994.
P	*Paradise* (1998) New York: Vintage, 1999.
PiD	*Playing in the Dark: Whiteness and the Literary Imagination.* 1992; London: Picador, 1993.

R   "Recitatif." *Confirmation: An Anthology of African American Women.* Ed. Amiri Baraka and Amina Baraka. New York: Morrow, 1983. 243–66.

RJEP   *Race-ing Justice, En-gendering Power: Essays on Anita Hill, Clarence Thomas and the Construction of Social Reality.* New York: Pantheon, 1992.

S   *Sula* (1973) New York: Vintage, 2005.

SoS   *Song of Solomon* (1977) New York: Vintage, 2005.

TB   *Tar Baby* (1981) New York: Vintage, 2004.

TG   Taylor-Guthrie, Danille, ed. *Conversations with Toni Morrison.* Jackson: University Press of Mississippi, 1994.

UTU   "Unspeakable Things Unspoken: The Afro-American Presence in American Literature." *Michigan Quarterly Review 28* (1989): 1–34.

WMM   *What Moves at the Margin: Selected Nonfiction.* Ed. Carolyn Denard. Jackson: University Press of Mississippi, 2008.

Chapter 1

Life

Speaking after the Cincinnati premiere of the opera *Margaret Garner* in 2005, Morrison recounted being told that she had won the Nobel Prize. A colleague from Princeton had called her early in the morning with the news, which was broadcast on television before Morrison had even been told. That afternoon, the chair of the selection committee called her from Stockholm to confirm the award. "Could you put that in writing?" Morrison asked the judge, and it was not until the decision came through on the fax machine that she really believed it was true. "I mean, you know," she told her Cincinnati audience, "I'm just a girl from Lorain."

So much you need to know about Toni Morrison is contained within that anecdote, not least her humorous-and-yet-dignified mode of self-presentation. To think of her as "just a girl from Lorain" is of course absurd – she could never be "just" anything – and yet her birthplace, which then became the setting for *The Bluest Eye*, is an unquantifiable part of who she is. And it is one of the paradoxes of her life story that, having risen to a position of huge success and wealth from humble origins and through gifts cultivated by immense hard work and sacrifice, her life story embodies the archetypal "American Dream" that her own novels subject to such skeptical scrutiny. There is to date no full-length authorized biography of Morrison to direct you to, no formal autobiography, and no published volumes of letters or diaries. There are, however, many wonderful interviews in which the author talks thoughtfully and in striking detail about her life and its relationship to her work. There are also the recent forewords to the Vintage editions of the novels, each of which gives a tantalizing glimpse of a different period in her life, and of its relationship to the novel being prefaced. Put together they do constitute life story of sorts. There already exist, as well, several biographical essays and chronologies of Morrison's life and career; all of these have informed the account that I give here.[1]

The following sketch of Toni Morrison's life is divided into four sections. The first is an account of her childhood and formal education, concluding with the completion of her master's degree at Cornell University In 1955. The second examines her two decades of teaching, editing, writing, and mothering up to the landmark success that greeted the publication of *Song of Solomon* in 1977. The third covers the period of consolidating literary and critical achievements, including the publication of *Beloved* in 1987 and *Jazz* and *Playing in the Dark* in 1992. These are her early years in an endowed chair at Princeton University, culminating in the winning of the Nobel Prize in 1993. The final section considers post-Nobel Toni Morrison, taking in the publication of *Paradise* (1998), *Love* (2003), and *A Mercy* (2008). While my account goes only as far as 2011, the year in which she turned eighty, it also looks forward to the publication of her tenth novel, *Home*, in May 2012.

1931–1955

Lorain, Ohio, in 1931, when Morrison was born to parents who had both migrated from the South as children, was a small, typical Rust Belt town. The author has often joked about being "a child of the Depression," has talked about having to move at least six times in search of cheaper rent as a child, and has described her family as "very poor." Her father, George Wofford, was from Georgia, and during Morrison's childhood he held down several jobs consecutively, including working as a welder at the nearby U.S. Steel plant, in order to support his four children. Morrison's mother, Ella Ramah Wofford (née Willis), had moved to Lorain with her own parents; they had come from Alabama via Kentucky. Morrison's maternal grandparents, Ardelia and John Solomon Willis, were hugely influential figures in her life. The author has frequently referred, as well, to the fact that John's mother (Morrison's great-grandmother) was Native American. It is surely significant that minor characters in her fiction often share the first names of real relatives: in *Beloved*, for example, one of Baby Suggs's lost children is called Ardelia. In *Song of Solomon*, meanwhile, Milkman discovers himself to be of mixed Native and African-American heritage. The novelist's weaving of the details of her life into her art indicates her deeply held conviction that an individual's experiences and the nation's history, or the personal and the political, are inextricably bound.

Morrison's name at her birth was Chloe Ardelia Wofford. While "Morrison" became her surname at her marriage in 1958, there is no consensus about how she became known as "Toni." According to the *New Yorker* journalist Hilton Als, when aged twelve she converted to Roman Catholicism and chose "Antony" as her baptismal name (*GiA* 67). She has told other sources, however, that "Toni" became her nickname when she was a young adult.[2] Chloe was her parents' second child and second daughter, to be followed by two brothers, and Morrison has often spoken of her close relationship with her elder sister, Lois. Her mother was an active member of the local African Methodist Episcopal

Church and its choir. "She sang, my mother, the way other people muse," writes Morrison. "Ave Maria, gratia plena ... I woke up this morning with an awful aching head / My new man has left me just a room and a bed ... Precious Lord, lead me on" (*J* xiii). Meanwhile her grandfather played the violin, and all the adults in her life were avid storytellers and conversationalists. They "could move easily into the language of the King James Bible and then back to standard English, and then segue into language that we would call street," Morrison recalled in 1996 (*DC* 131). This culturally rich environment – the music, the storytelling, the central place of the Bible, and the close-knit nature of her family – is an obvious and profound presence in Morrison's work.

The author was the only African-American student in her first grade class, and her neighborhood was anything but uniformly black. The town's population was diverse due to immigrants from Southern and Eastern Europe who also worked at U.S. Steel; Morrison says this made her "sensitive to languages very early" (*DC* 203, 131). Despite the mixed nature of her milieu, however, as Morrison has wryly observed, the adults who raised her held "widely disparate and sometimes conflicting views" about race. Her parents "differed about whether the moral fiber of white people would ever improve" (*WMM* 6). The author "grew up with a complicated notion of the South, neither sentimental nor wholly frightening": her mother was "nostalgic" but never returned there; her father "recounted vividly the violence he had seen at first-hand from White southerners" but "went back to Georgia every year" (*DC* 178).

Race relations in Lorain itself were no less complicated. In *The Bluest Eye* (1970), Morrison describes the town and its Lake Erie shore as a "melting pot on the lip of America facing the cold but receptive Canada," a town that "boasted an affinity with Oberlin," the underground railroad station and site of the college to which Denver is heading at the end of *Beloved* (*BE* 91). Yet that first novel's subject is the many-layered, deeply ingrained racist culture of the town in the very years of Morrison's childhood. Her father maintained a lifelong suspicion of white people, and at least once she witnessed him attacking a white man whom he believed to be a threat to the children, whereas her mother judged every individual on his or her individual merits (*WMM* 6). These conflicting perspectives perhaps explain her acute authorial sensitivity to the complexities and ambiguities of racialized cultural formations and racist attitudes.

Morrison was an outstanding student at school and has been an avid reader for as long as she can remember. She devoured canonical classics from a very young age; she has described books as a "driving thing" in her childhood and has made specific mention of Tolstoy, Dostoevsky, Jane Austen, and Theodore Dreiser, among others (*DC* 100). She came later to African-American and African literatures, which perhaps affected her all the more because she discovered them late. During her teenage years she worked as a helper at the

Lorain Public Library, a site of great importance to her, at which, in 1995, she opened the Toni Morrison Reading Room. She also began after-school domestic cleaning work from the age of "around thirteen" (*DC* 100). At Lorain High School she worked on the school newspaper and yearbook, graduating with honors and with ambitions to become a dancer.[3] In her foreword to *Love*, Morrison reflects on the invaluable resources of her childhood – "a feisty mother, a supportive father, and insatiable reading habits" (*L* xii).

When Morrison went to Howard University in 1949, she was the first member of her family to attend college. She majored in English and minored in Classics, studying with veteran intellectuals of the Harlem Renaissance era such as Alain Locke and Sterling Brown. The Classics Department at this time was under the chairmanship of Frank Snowden Jr., whose lifelong scholarly interest was the role of Africans in ancient Greece and Rome. Morrison has, however, frequently remarked on her surprise at and discomfort with the conservative social and racial atmosphere she encountered at Howard. It was "middle class" and "upwardly mobile," she observed in 1985; when she asked to write a paper on "Black Characters in Shakespeare," the English Department were "very alarmed (*TG* 174–5)," and there was a pervasive culture of categorizing students according to the lightness or darkness of their skin. A highlight of her undergraduate years, on the other hand, was her involvement with the theater group, the Howard Players. Touring the Deep South with that group was one of the defining experiences of her life.

The years during which Morrison studied for her master's degree in English at Cornell –1953–5 – are ones she has spoken of very little. What we do know is about the thesis she wrote there: entitled "Virginia Woolf's and William Faulkner's Treatment of the Alienated," it discusses the representation of suicide by these authors with whom her own fictional style clearly has much in common, and to whom she is now frequently compared by critics. The thesis is also notable for its interest in the influence of Greek tragedy on Faulkner; in her own novels she went on to engage with those same conventions. When she completed her master's degree she was still only twenty-four years old. But from 2245 Elyria Avenue, Lorain, Ohio, in 1931 to Graduation Day at Cornell University, Ithaca, New York, in 1955 – that must have felt, already, like quite some journey to have made.

1955–1977

After graduating from Cornell, Morrison took the first of the many teaching posts she was to hold: at Texas Southern University. In 1957 she moved back to

Washington, D.C., and to Howard, this time as a teacher. Although she stayed there until 1964, she felt no less ambivalent about the culture there than she had a decade earlier. "Those were the pre–Civil Rights years," she explained in 1985, "the years when the measure of excellence was to outstrip the white schools at one thing or another" (*DC* 32). In 1963 she joined a writing group at Howard, for which she began work on a short story that was to become the foundation of *The Bluest Eye*. Other members of the group included the writer Claude Brown (still a student at that time), the playwright and director Owen Dodson, and the painter Charles Sebree, whom Morrison remembers telling her, after reading her story, "*You* are a writer" (*GiA* 69).

In 1958, Morrison (or Wofford, as she still was) had married a Jamaican architect, Harold Morrison. Their first son, Harold Ford, was born in 1961, but the marriage was not a happy one. Morrison has spoken little of her ex-husband – "I can't be honest without causing somebody pain, mostly my children," she said in 1976 (*DC* 4) – and they divorced after traveling in Europe together in 1964. Morrison has said she was a "constant nuisance" during her marriage because she was not "subservient" (*TG* 51); "he knew better about his life but not about mine," she said in 1992 (*DC* 72). After parting company from her husband she returned to her family in Lorain, Ohio, where her second son, Slade Kevin, was born. In 1965, against her parents' wishes, she moved with her young boys to Syracuse, upstate New York, to take a job as a senior editor for the textbook publisher L. W. Singer, which was a subsidiary of Random House. With hindsight Morrison puts a positive gloss on this period of her life, but it was obviously a profoundly challenging one. In 1992, she reflected, "I had to stop and say, let me start again and see what it is like to be a grown up" (*DC* 72).

During the bleak couple of years Morrison lived in Syracuse, she spent her evenings expanding her story into *The Bluest Eye*. After putting in full days at the office, and when her children were in bed, she "didn't have anyone to talk to" so she "wrote it as a way to talk" (*DC* 7). This is also when she developed the habit of getting up to write before dawn, "to use the time before [the children] said "Mama" (*DC* 64). She states that she wrote the first book "because it wasn't there"; it was the kind of book she wanted to read, and creating the first novel felt "like a very long, sustained, reading process" (*DC* 69, 46). After being rejected by numerous publishers, *The Bluest Eye* was published (in a small print run of 2,000 hardback copies) by Holt, Rinehart, Winston in 1970. By this time Morrison was working for Random House in New York City; she had moved there in 1968 to a job in the scholastic division and then became a senior trade editor working for Jason Epstein. Although she made little of her own writing to her editorial colleagues, Robert Gottlieb of Knopf (also an imprint of Random House) became her own editor at this time and has worked with her on every novel except *Jazz* and *Paradise* since then.

Morrison lived in Queens during the late 1960s and early 1970s, commuting daily to her Manhattan office, and also teaching in 1971–2 at SUNY Purchase. The picture she paints of this time (particularly in her foreword to *Sula*) is one of financial hardship and childcare difficulties, of a closely knit network of like-minded women friends, of joy in intellectual discovery (of many African authors, for example), of significant achievements in her editorial work, and of political engagement and "daring." *Sula* was published in 1973, and throughout that decade, in a racial climate that was unreceptive, Morrison's influence in the publication of black writing was unparalleled. The material she edited and publicized includes the fiction of Toni Cade Bambara, Leon Forrest, and Gayl Jones; the poetry of Lucille Clifton and June Jordan; and the autobiographies of Angela Davis, Muhammad Ali, and Huey Newton (*B* ix). She also published anthologies of little-known "third world" writing such as *Contemporary African Literature* in 1972 and *Giant Talk* in 1975.[4]

Perhaps the editorial project that has had the most profound influence on Morrison herself was *The Black Book*, published in 1974 with Middleton Harris as its lead editor. This is a documentary history of the African-American experience, consisting of newspaper articles, letters, speeches, photographs, folk songs, and other cultural memorabilia that span three hundred years. In her seminal article on the project, "Rediscovering Black History" (1974), Morrison describes it as "unconventional history told from the point of view of everyday people" and explains the motivation behind it as the attempt to recover some of the values lost through the civil rights movement: "those qualities of resistance, excellence and integrity" (*WMM* 55, 42). As is now well known, it is here that Morrison first encountered the newspaper clipping about Margaret Garner, the historical forerunner to Sethe in *Beloved*. The author has written of the "despair" she felt while compiling the materials (which include two photos of her mother) – "it was like growing up black one more time" – and also of the "joy" (*WMM* 44; 49). In 2009, Random House reissued the book in a 35th Anniversary Edition.

In September 1975, Morrison's father died. She has described the period following as one of "unimaginable sadness" in which she struggled to accept not only the loss of him but "the loss of the person he thought [she] was" (*SoS* ix, x). In 1977, and frequently since, she has recalled the way he taught her to take pride in her work through the fact that he soldered his name, unseen by anyone else, on every "perfect seam" he welded on ships (*DC* 14). The positive outcome to the "big void" that he left was that she started writing "a book that was about men" (*WMM* 80): the result, published in 1977 and dedicated to "Daddy," was *Song of Solomon*.

1977–1993

Song of Solomon was Morrison's first major public success. Soon after its appearance it was chosen as a main selection for the Book-of-the-Month Club; it was the first African-American text to be recognized in this way since Richard Wright's *Native Son* in 1940. In 1978 it won both the National Book Critics' Circle Award and the American Academy and Institute of Arts and Letters Award. At this time, Morrison found that publishing "became less interesting" to her as her hands-on editorial work diminished, and as the books she had brought out did not sell well (*DC* 204; *TG* 133). Devoting more time to her teaching (which now included visiting lectureships at Yale, at Rutgers, and – in 1986 – at Bard), and primarily to her writing, she began to go to the Random House office on only one day a week. She wrote the foreword to the Billops/ Dodson/Van der Zee collaboration *The Harlem Book of the Dead* (1978) at this time;[5] one of the Van der Zee photographs and its backstory became the inspiration for *Jazz* (*J* ix). In 1988 Morrison reflected that after she wrote *Solomon* she "began to think of [herself] legally as a writer" (*DC* 46). After that novel's commercial success, she bought the converted boathouse on the Hudson River, in Rockland County, New York, that has been her principal home ever since.

In 1981 Morrison published her fourth novel, *Tar Baby*. The novel was inspired, she tells us in its foreword, by her grandmother, who "needed her dreams," and for whom she used to make up stories (*TB* 14). By now honors were bestowed on an annual basis: this year she was elected to the American Academy and Institute of Arts and Letters (who had named her a "distinguished writer" in 1977), and in 1980 she had been appointed to the National Council of the Arts. In 1983 she published (in a collection edited by Amiri and Amina Baraka) her one and only short story, "Recitatif," but continued to downplay her many activities and achievements. "I really only do two things" she told Nellie McKay in an interview that same year. "All my work has to do with books. I teach books, write books, edit books, or talk about books. ... And the only other thing I do is raise my children" (*TG* 140). Nevertheless, by the end of 1983 she had resigned from her position at Random House. It was during the ensuing period of newly found freedom that she began work on her fifth and most famous novel: *Beloved*. As she explains, "A few days after my last day at work ... I sat on the porch,

... looking at giant stones piled up to take the river's occasional fist. ...
She walked up out of the water, climbed the rocks, and leaned against the
gazebo. Nice hat" (*B* x–xii).

In 1984, Morrison was named to the Alfred Schweitzer Professorship at
SUNY Albany, which she held until 1986. While there she wrote and assisted
in the production of the play *Dreaming Emmett*, which was staged in collaboration with the director Gilbert Moses in January 1986 (see Chapter 2, "Other
Creative Work"). In its chorus-like collection of ghosts from Emmett Till's past
and its preoccupation with revenge, it anticipates the thematic concerns of
Beloved. And that novel, published in 1987 and winning the Pulitzer in 1988,
marks a watershed moment in Morrison's life: it consolidated her success and
won her international fame. From that point on, she became a key player on
the global cultural stage.

In 1985, Morrison had told Gloria Naylor, "I think ... I won't write anything
after *Beloved*" (*TG* 212). In 1989, when appointed to the Robert Goheen Chair
in the Council of the Humanities at Princeton University, she became the first
African-American woman to hold an endowed chair at an Ivy League univer-
sity. Her lecturing and publications continued apace: she delivered the Tanner
Lecture at the University of Michigan in 1988 (published as "Unspeakable
Things Unspoken," 1989), the Massey Lectures at Harvard in 1990, and the
Clark Lectures at Trinity College, Cambridge, in the same year. Both the
Harvard and Cambridge lectures were to become the groundbreaking work
of literary criticism *Playing in the Dark*, published in 1992. In the same year
Morrison published her sixth novel, *Jazz*, which she has often cited as her own
favorite, and which became a *New York Times* best seller. She also formalized
her role as a social commentator, editing the essay collection *Race-ing Justice,
En-gendering Power* (1992).

Speaking about her writing habits in a 1992 interview, Morrison said, "I
always get up and make a cup of coffee while it is still dark ... and then I drink
the coffee and watch the light come. ... This ritual comprises my preparation
to enter a space that I can only call non-secular" (*DC* 65). Such a routine was
presumably a necessity given the achievements and demands of this period
in her life, but its symbolism also sets a spiritual tenor that Morrison herself
was to continue. On 7 October 1993 she was awarded the Nobel Prize in literature. According to the *Washington Post*, on that day she had unplugged the
phone by 10:00 am and taught her Princeton class as normal. At the award
ceremony in Stockholm, in December of the same year, after delivering her
fabulous lecture, she closed her acceptance speech by asking us to share with
her "a moment of grace" (*NL* 33).

Since 1993

Just weeks after the Nobel award ceremony, Morrison's home on the Hudson River burned down. The fire broke out on the morning of Christmas Day, in 1993, and in September 1994 the author revealed to a *New York Times* interviewer that she might "not ever, ever, ever get over" the loss of her "photographs, ... children's report cards [and] manuscripts," as well as treasured first editions of Emily Dickinson, William Faulkner, and a second edition of Frederick Douglass published in England (*DC* 103; 153). Two months later, Morrison's mother died. The author refused to perceive these "very serious devastations" as a manifestation of the so-called curse of the Nobel, however, preferring to identify the prize as the distinguishing positive event of this time (*DC* 103). In 1994 she founded a new performing arts seminar program, the Princeton Atelier, and at this time she herself was writing lyrics for works by the composers André Previn, Richard Danielpour, Max Roach, and Judith Weir, many of which were performed at Carnegie Hall. Meanwhile her teaching at Princeton centered on her twelve-lecture course American Africanism, which she taught for six years, along with Creative Writing.

In 1998, Morrison co-edited (with Claudia Brodsky Lacour) a collection of essays on the O. J. Simpson case entitled *Birth of A Nation'hood*. In her now-established role as a public intellectual or spokesperson for the Left, in the *New Yorker* she criticized the "raw comedy spiked with Cotton Mather homilies" that characterized the pursuit of President Clinton in 1998 (*WMM* 152) and helped to organize an intellectuals' protest against his impeachment; was scathing in interviews some years later about the Bush administration's response to the Al-Qaeda attacks, and gave speeches at Howard and Princeton on the future of university education.

In 1998 Morrison published her seventh novel, *Paradise*, which completed the trilogy beginning with *Beloved* and *Jazz*. Between 2002 and 2003 she published (together with her son Slade) the three children's books in the *Who's Got Game?* series, a graphic-text-style revision of Aesop; and in 2003 she published her eighth novel, *Love*. Throughout this period she maintained an intense schedule of international book tours (speaking at the Oxford Union about *Paradise* in May 1998, for example), public readings, and media appearances. She has always been willing to engage with her readership, both general and scholarly, and is profoundly invested in the reception of her work. She has, for example, regularly attended the conferences of the Toni Morrison Society, which was founded by Carolyn Denard in 1993.[6] At these events in Lorain, Ohio, in 2000; in Washington, D.C., in 2003; and in Cincinnati in 2005 (which included the state premiere of the opera *Margaret Garner*, for which she had written the libretto), she both gave formal presentations and participated informally in scholarly panels. At the Paris conference in 2010, besides her scheduled appearances, she sat in for several hours on the roundtable discussion about the teaching of her work.

Honors and tributes, both formal and informal, have accumulated rapidly since 1993 and the Nobel. In 1996 she was awarded the National Book Foundation Medal for Distinguished Contribution to American Letters; *The Dancing Mind* was her acceptance speech in November of that year. She received an honorary doctoral degree from the École Normale Supérieure in 2003; in 2005 from the University of Oxford; and in 2006 from the Sorbonne. At the same time, Oprah Winfrey's nomination of four Morrison novels for her book club – *Solomon* in 1996, *Paradise* in 1998, *The Bluest Eye* in 2000, and *Sula* in 2002 – had a major impact on the author's popularity and sales. Her seventieth birthday in 2001, and her seventy-fifth in 2006, were marked by celebrations at the New York Public Library and at the Lincoln Center, respectively.

In June 2006 Morrison transferred her professorial status at Princeton to emerita, but in no sense of the word did she "retire" from the world of work. She spent the period from October of that year to January 2007 as guest curator at the Musée du Louvre in Paris, where she organized a series of events and curatorial processes that centered on the theme "Étranger Chez Soi," or "The Foreigner's Home," while in March 2007, back in New York, she curated the "Art Is Otherwise" event at the Baryshnikov Arts Center. With hindsight, the year 2008 reads as one in which Morrison's literary endeavors and political goals (a distinction she herself would never contemplate) complemented and fulfilled each other in striking ways. In January of that year, she wrote a public letter endorsing Barack Obama, who was competing against Hillary Clinton in the primaries. In July, Morrison attended the Toni Morrison Society Conference in Charleston, South Carolina, which included the ceremonial placing of a memorial "Bench by the Road" on Sullivan's Island.[7] Her ninth novel, *A Mercy*, was published in November of 2008, just days after the election of Obama to the presidency.

In 2009 Morrison edited the PEN anti-censorship collection *Burn this Book*, to which she also contributed the introductory essay. On the opening day of the Toni Morrison Society Conference in Paris (4 November 2010), Morrison was presented with France's Legion d'Honneur. The next day she presided at the placing of another "bench by the road," and on the last day she read the opening passage from her then-unfinished novel, *Home* (May 2012), although she did not reveal its title as such until her reading (following the placing of a further bench) at George Washington University in September 2011. Just a few weeks after the Paris conference, in December 2010, Morrison's younger son, Slade, with whom she had collaborated on many children's books, suddenly passed away. This tragedy did not prevent her going ahead, however, with her eightieth birthday celebration, held by the Toni Morrison Society at the Library of Congress, on 18 February 2011. This was attended by numerous people of significance in her personal and professional lives, both past and present.

At the eightieth birthday event, Morrison was presented with a Festschrift, *Memory and Meaning: Essays in Honour of Toni Morrison*.[8] The title of this work illuminates the importance of both cultural and individual memory in her work, recalling as it does her seminal essay "The Site of Memory" (1987). That essay's testimony to Morrison's own sense of the inextricability of her life, of her writing, and of the high-stake politics of both, was confirmed by the many memories, stories, and tributes that the eightieth birthday celebration involved. My own memory of Morrison on that occasion is a fitting way to close this unfinished story of her life. Clearly in a state of grief and not in the best physical health, she addressed the gathering from a wheelchair, talking about what the day meant to her. She spoke of Jessye Norman's singing as "a great comfort," of the "stunning" way that the scholarship on her work had changed since 1970, and of the fact that turning eighty was "really something." "You know," she said, "sixty? Yeah, that's OK. Seventy? Hmmm, that's all right. But eighty? That's, well, that's ... pow!" And she punched the air.

Chapter 2

Works

Introduction to the Fiction

One of Morrison's favorite metaphors to describe her fictional project is that of the house and home. "If I had to live in a racial house," she wrote in the landmark essay "Home" (1997), "it was important ... to rebuild it so that it was not a windowless prison into which I was forced, ... but rather an open house" (*H* 4). In this image, the "house" in need of rebuilding stands for many things at once: for mainstream American ideology, for the national literary canon, for the genre of the novel, and even for language itself. The challenge Morrison sets herself is to transform these flawed but powerful structures, and to create a better version of reality that she conceives of as "home." The title of her most recent novel, *Home*, therefore comes as no surprise. From the very beginning of her writing career, from the early 1960s when she was working on the short story that was to become *The Bluest Eye*, she set out quite deliberately and self-consciously to create literature that was different from what had gone before.

Morrison writes slowly, with great forethought and deliberation. She reworks her drafts until she is completely satisfied, and until the writing appears "effortless" (*TG* 123). The result is a dense, allusive prose that demands to be read aloud and that richly repays rereading and close analysis. Paradoxically, it is the complex layeredness of her writing that, on the one hand, makes her an obvious comparison with other innovators such as Joyce, Woolf, Ellison, Faulkner, and Bambara, and that, on the other, ensures the uniqueness of her vision and of her voice. In her foreword to *Sula*, Morrison describes her "sensibility" as "highly political *and* passionately aesthetic" (*S* xi). As far as she is concerned, aesthetic integrity and political effectiveness are inseparable, and to try to distinguish the way something is written from the influence it has is nonsensical and futile. When setting out on a study of this author, it is essential always to bear in mind that the unifying impulse in her work – that of perpetually taking preexisting cultural structures apart and revising, rewriting, reenvisioning, or rebuilding them into new and better forms – is always and already both an artistic and a political process.

To state the obvious, Morrison's subject is the African-American experience. Put together chronologically (by subject matter rather than in order of publication), her ten novels examine key moments of American history. While centering on late twentieth-century life, *Love* and *Tar Baby* also play with ideas of the continent's discovery and colonization; *A Mercy* opens up new perspectives on late seventeenth-century New England; *Beloved* has come to be seen as the defining literary treatment of slavery; *Jazz* deals with Reconstruction, black migration, and urbanization; and *Paradise* is simultaneously about the early twentieth-century phenomenon of the all-black town and the founding of the United States itself. *The Bluest Eye* and *Sula* epitomize small-town life in the depressed decades in which they are set (the 1930s and 1940s), while the action of *Home* and *Song of Solomon* is rooted in the fraught battles over racial and sexual equality that characterized the American 1950s–60s. But despite the primacy of history in these works, and the vital energy imbued by Morrison's commitment to the disruption of white patriarchal "History," the books are anything but conventionally understood "historical novels." Morrison has written of "the personal that is always embedded in the public" (*H* 12), and her way into political conflict and debate is always through the inner struggles of fully realized individual characters. The author once said that though she could not change the future, she knew she could change the past. The way she does this is to approach that past through the personal lives of those whom the dominant culture has silenced, erased, or forgotten: an ugly black schoolgirl in *The Bluest Eye*, the servants in a millionaire's mansion in *Tar Baby*, a formerly enslaved mother in *Beloved*, women abused as children in *Love*.

It may surprise some readers to learn that the extent to which it is possible, or even useful, to categorize Morrison as a feminist writer is a matter of ongoing critical controversy. Despite the fact that girls and women, and their relationships with each other, are so consistently at the center of the author's imagined worlds, she herself has often rejected the label of "feminist." She has frequently expressed her sense of the "problematic" nature of "white feminist views," in that they ignore (and even exploit) the specific needs of black women, and has observed that "the enemy is not men. The enemy is the concept of patriarchy" (*DC* 34). She "would never write any … 'ist' novels," she says, because she "can't take positions that are closed" (*DC* 141). While passionately committed to exploring the experience of girlhood or motherhood, or women's vulnerability to sexual violence, or the specific educational and employment problems faced by black women, she maintains that to substitute matriarchy for patriarchy is no solution. In my discussion of the contexts of her work in the third chapter of this book, therefore, I have not treated "feminism" as a distinct section. The Morrisonian worldview resists and counteracts any compartmentalization of women's experience, despite (or, as she would argue, because of) the authorial investment in it.

It is Morrison's attention to the voices of the marginalized, of the "disremembered and unaccounted for," that gives rise to the narrative structures of her novels (*B* 323). Rather than presenting a conventional chronological version of events told from a single standpoint, she combines multiple viewpoints or voices with disrupted chronologies and strategic withholding of information so that the picture is always evolving, always revealing something new. Sometimes a voice in the first person opens a novel (for example, in *Jazz* or *A Mercy*). Other times an apparently authoritative third-person beginning lulls the reader into a false sense of security (for example, in the openings of *Song of Solomon* or *Paradise*). The author has said many times that "the *meaning* of a novel is in its structure" (*DC* 218). Her overt rationale behind her technique is to achieve a new kind of realism – to represent experience as we actually perceive it. But there is surely more at stake in her novelistic form than this. "I knew from the beginning that I could not, would not, reproduce the master's voice and its assumptions of the all-knowing law of the white father," she has said (*H* 4). Her dismantling of conventional narrative chronology and viewpoint is one of the crucial means by which she dismantles "the master's voice."

A third effect of Morrison's polyphonic, nonlinear methods is that they demand readers' participation in the creation of meaning. I would urge you not to read her recent forewords to the novels before you have read the novels themselves, because to some extent they tell you what to think about the novels, and they diminish her prior insistence on active reading that is part of her political strategy. To be participatory readers creates us as a community of readers, implicates us in event, and also places Morrison's work firmly within the African-American tradition of "call and response." Morrison has spoken of her aim to create an author/reader relationship analogous to the protagonist/ chorus relationship in Greek tragedy, to the preacher/congregation relationship in church, and to the soloist/group relationship in jazz (*TG* 176).

The analogy between Morrison's literary technique and jazz is by now well worn, not least because she has made it so frequently herself, but it is no less compelling for that. It is important to recognize, as well, that this is a comparison that has many elements to it and that each one clarifies a different aspect of Morrisonian style. Writing about her mother, in 2004, the author recalls, "Like the music that came to be known as Jazz, she took from everywhere, knew everything – gospel, classic, blues, hymns – and made it her own" (*J* xiii). This would be an equally valid comment on the author's own approach to life and art; her novels are remarkable for the sheer breadth of literatures, traditions, mythologies, and other cultural resources on which they draw. Some critics have tended to polarize their interpretations of her allusiveness. For example, it is not unusual to claim that the influences on her writing are somehow either "African" or "European" but not both, or that one cultural influence is more significant than the other. To adhere to such binary division, however; to insist that Morrison and her readers must make "either/or" choices, is simply to falsify the fiction. Morrison herself has spoken of the limits of the "dichotomous double consciousness," and of the attractions of a "concrete thrill of borderlessness," and of "difference that is prized but unprivileged" (*H* 9, 11). African, American, African-American, Native American, and European traditions are all synthesized, made her own, in her hands.

A third level on which the jazz analogy works is in terms of audience and appeal. In a 1994 interview, Morrison pointed out that jazz music was at once "very complicated, very sophisticated, ... very difficult" and "also very popular." She strives for her own fiction to encompass this duality: to "be as demanding and sophisticated as I want it to be, and at the same time be accessible in a sort of emotional way to lots of people, just like jazz" (*DC*106). This is something that in many ways she has achieved; in America she is a household name, and yet she writes some of the most demanding literature on the market.

Ten novels on, is it possible to trace development in the progress of the oeuvre, or commonalities between the works? Morrison's subjects are trauma, violence, pain, and loss. Yet there is clearly a move away from the unrelenting bleakness of the end of *The Bluest Eye*, or the "circles and circles of sorrow" that bring *Sula* to a close (*S* 174). In the trilogy, after the indeterminate endings of *Song of Solomon* and *Tar Baby*, there is a repeated emphasis on survival, and on the "some kind of tomorrow" for which Paul D and Sethe long (*B* 322). And there is also humor. It may sound odd to say that Morrison, whose subject matter is so serious, is a profoundly humorous and witty writer, but it is true. Through irony, parody, pastiche, and characters' sense of the comic, the author suggests that humor is what makes endurance and survival possible, but that it does not trivialize its subject. "Laughter is serious," realizes Violet in *Jazz*, "more complicated, more serious than tears" (113).

So, if you are just setting out on a study of Morrison's novels, you can expect to find great riches. There are heroic, resilient characters who face extreme historically influenced circumstances; psychological insights and knowledge of the human heart that will make you nod in recognition; worlds in which myth and magic, spiritual faith and the forces of the irrational, are respected; close attention to the physical pleasures of life such as food and sex; language that is strange and compelling, that is "speakerly, aural, colloquial" and beautiful (*BE* 172); imagery that is new and surprising but always apt; a cultural allusiveness that is dazzling in its scope; and a metafictional, postmodern quality in which the nature of a story's telling is always part of its subject. Morrison is of course not a perfect writer. There are passages that are overwritten, there are moments of cliché, there is withholding of information that is occasionally just frustrating, and there are occasional flashes of didacticism. But her triumph is in the fact that her vision of the political realities of African-American life is simultaneously a vision of all humanity. She makes the specific universal, without ever diminishing the political force of her specificity. Her fiction is a place where "race both matters and is rendered impotent," and as a result she has achieved what she set out to do: "to transform this house completely" (*H* 4).

The Bluest Eye (1970)

Morrison's first novel tells the agonizing life story of Pecola Breedlove, an African-American girl from a poor and dysfunctional family who is eleven years old when the action of the book begins. The setting is Lorain, Ohio (Morrison's own birthplace), and the key events – Pecola's being bullied at school, despised by the community, rejected by her mother, raped by her father, and manipulated by a quack healer – take place between 1940 and 1941. The principal narrator is Pecola's school friend Claudia MacTeer, whose voice alternates between her adult perspective, looking back at the past, and a version of her perspective as a child, encountering each moment as it occurs.

First and foremost, this is a book about racism, about what it is like to grow up in a racist culture, and about what Morrison terms the "racial self-loathing" that such a culture engenders (*BE* foreword np). It is a book primarily about the causes and devastating consequences of intraracial racism, of the ways in which some Americans of African descent grow to look down on and despise others in accordance with an insidious, destructive value system in which categorization and discrimination (strategies learned from whites' oppression of blacks) are the key weapons. Pecola's profound sense of worthlessness develops in response to dominant cultural notions of "romantic love" and "physical beauty," which Morrison describes as "probably the most destructive ideas in the history of human thought" (*BE* 95). The townsfolk's conception of "beauty" is shaped by popular culture's privileging of the conventional traits of white glamour – blonde hair and blue eyes – exemplified by the white goddesses of the silver screen whom this depression era community wish to emulate.

The novel's title refers to the fact that in the last stages of her sanity, or the beginning stages of her insanity, Pecola pays a visit to the healer Soaphead Church and begs him to give her blue eyes. The penultimate section of the book depicts the girl's consciousness split into two voices that discuss the prettiness of the new eyes she believes she has acquired, interwoven with fractured allusions to the traumatic experiences she has undergone. As with every Morrisonian title, *The Bluest Eye* is one that works on several levels. While blue eyes function as a synecdoche for a value system that shores up white superiority and power, the pun on "blue" in the sense of sadness is obvious, linking to a similar pun on "tear" in Claudia's surname, "MacTeer." The "bluest" also connotes the blues, an original African-American musical form that expresses both suffering and survival at its core. The blues migrated from the rural South to the urban North along with the many thousands of black people who are the historical counterparts to Pecola's parents, Cholly and Pauline (born in Georgia and Alabama, respectively), who met in Kentucky, and who moved together to Ohio. The "eye" of the book's title not only expresses its thematic preoccupation with ways of seeing, but also puns on "I," suggesting Pecola's eroded sense of self and complete lack of self-esteem. The disintegration of herself, of the "I," works in direct counterpoint to mainstream American ideologies of individualism and empowered selfhood.

The novel's structure is complex; it is initially baffling, and deliberately so. The experimental narrative technique and the book's disjointed form are key to Morrison's concern with the ways racial and racist codes are embedded in the narratives and the language that we create, and that we are at the same time created by. Besides the shifting perspectives of Claudia, there is an omniscient third-person narrative voice that relates the life histories of Pecola's impoverished and downtrodden parents, of Soaphead Church, and of Geraldine, the upwardly mobile woman who calls Pecola "a nasty little black bitch" as she expels her from her house (*BE* 72). But the work's innovative beginning is a parodic quotation from one of the so-called Dick and Jane readers. These were a series of elementary school books, devised by Zerna Sharp and William Gray and published by Foreman and Co., which from 1930 onward were widely used to teach American children to read. The passage Morrison quotes begins as follows:

> Here is the house. It is green and white. It has a red door. It is very pretty. Here is the family. Mother, Father, Dick and Jane live in the green-and-white house. They are very happy. (*BE* 1)

In *The Bluest Eye*, this passage – which prefaces (in excerpted form) each section describing the Breedloves' lives – stands as the ur-text of the ideology that has come to be called "whiteness." It epitomizes the mythological perfect home and family to which all Americans are supposed to aspire and yet that many are prevented from achieving by the very same system that promotes the myth. Morrison reveals the extent to which children were brainwashed, in that as they learned to read they also absorbed the message that middle-class white culture was the only valuable and desirable standard.

The voice following the initial "Dick and Jane" quotation is that of Claudia's adulthood, which begins the first of the novel's four structuring seasons, "Autumn." "*Quiet as it's kept,*" she confides in us, "*there were no marigolds in the fall of 1941. We thought, at the time, that it was because Pecola was having her father's baby that the marigolds did not grow*" (*BE* 4). Morrison has said more about these two sentences, in public appearances and in her essays, than she has of any other lines in her oeuvre. In the afterword to the novel, for example, she analyzes the "conspiratorial" nature of "*quiet as it's kept*" and argues that the second sentence, in making the flowers more important than the incest, reveals the narrator to be a child (*BE* 169–70). The immediate announcement of the terrible fate of Pecola, the revelation of the plot's denouement at the novel's opening, is a deliberate disruption of conventional narrative technique. Claudia goes on to tell us, in this same opening passage, that "*Since* why *is difficult to handle, one must take refuge in* how" (*3*). The result of her opening disclosure is that when we finally arrive at the detailed description of Cholly's rape of his daughter, our focus is not on "what" happened but on "how" the assault came about, both physically and emotionally. This technique enables a second favorite Morrisonian narrative strategy: the depiction of multiple and conflicting perspectives on any one event.

Like the Breedloves, the MacTeers are materially poor, but unlike the Breedloves, they are emotionally rich. Mr. and Mrs. MacTeer, Claudia's parents, are loving, strict, in control, and protective of the narrator and her elder sister, Frieda. While Pecola is staying temporarily housed with MacTeers, she makes an impression on the two sisters, first, because she is transfixed by the blonde and blue-eyed Shirley Temple, and, second, because during her stay she has her first menstrual period. This moment symbolizes the transitional phase of the girls' lives, the beginning of adolescence and sexual awareness, and the end of their childhood innocence.

Claudia recalls that at this point she herself "had not yet arrived at the turning point in the development of [her] psyche that would allow [her] to love" Shirley Temple (13). In other words, she had not yet been brainwashed: she preferred the dark-haired actress Jane Withers, who in the 1934 film *Bright Eyes* threatens to attack Shirley Temple's doll. Claudia presumably identifies with Withers because she herself "destroyed white baby dolls" (*BE* 12). Given a "big, blue-eyed Baby Doll" for Christmas every year, instead of loving them she used to dismember each one, "to see of what it was made, to discover the dearness, to find the beauty" (14). These details not only symbolize the novel's dismemberment of the ideology of whiteness, but also allude to the ground-breaking "doll tests" carried out in the 1940s by the psychologists Kenneth B. Clark and Mamie Phipps Clark. The tests were designed to ascertain the psychological effects of segregation on black children, and in the "doll test" children were asked to identify the race of four dolls ranging in color from pale to dark, and to express a preference for one of them. The majority of children chose the white doll as their favorite, proving their perception of their own inferiority, and the Clarks' findings, published in a paper of 1950, were specifically quoted by the Supreme Court in their 1954 landmark decision about school desegregation (*Brown v. Board of Education*). *The Bluest Eye* is set in the very decade in which these tests were carried out, and the despised and self-hating Pecola would undoubtedly have selected the whitest doll.

In the "Winter" section, Morrison sets the scene of the Breedlove family's unhomelike home: the squalid storefront in which Pauline and Cholly endlessly fight, and in which the stove (in contrast to the roaring hearth in the MacTeers' house) never properly burns. Against this miserable, ugly backdrop, the author stages what she calls "a series of rejections" of Pecola: "some routine, some exceptional, some monstrous" (*BE* foreword np). First, in the grocery store, when Mr. Yacobowksi tries to take her money without touching her hand, the "inexplicable shame" she feels at his "distaste for her blackness" is erased only by the soothing picture of clean, blonde Mary Jane on the candy wrappers (*BE* 36–8). A few days later, when Frieda and Claudia rescue Pecola from a ring of schoolboy bullies, the unexpected attentions of the glamorous, pale-skinned classmate Maureen Peal temporarily mollify Pecola, but Maureen goes on to insult her new "friend" about her "old black daddy" (56).

The next character to exacerbate Pecola's sense of worthlessness and concomitant yearning for blue eyes is "sugar-brown" Geraldine (64), the socially aspirational mother of another classmate. According to the novel's anonymous, omniscient narrative voice, Geraldine is typical of a certain class of pale-skinned young African-American women who expend all their energy trying to eradicate "the dreadful funkiness of passion, the funkiness of nature" (64). She exemplifies intraracial discrimination at its most insidious. Because Pecola seems to represent all the dirt, poverty, and blackness from which Geraldine has spent her entire life running, Geraldine throws her out of her house with a racist insult while showing great concern for the injured cat.

Toward the start of the novel's longest section, "Spring," comes Pauline's rejection of her daughter – an act of breathtaking treachery. When Pecola upsets the piping hot cobbler, Pauline's only concern is for the floor she has just cleaned and for her employer's "pink-and-yellow" daughter (*BE* 85). As Pecola and the MacTeers are sent packing, the words "crazy fool … my floor

... my floor" burn "hotter and darker than the smoking berries" (85). Though Morrison does devote pages to explaining the struggles and disappointments of Pauline's life – her deformed foot from a childhood injury, a youth filled with housekeeping and child care responsibilities, her initial excitement on marrying Cholly, and their migration to Lorain followed by the demise of their relationship – readers commonly struggle to sympathize with her. Her infatuation with the myths of white beauty and happiness that is nurtured by the movies finds expression in her utter devotion to her white employer and to her domestic responsibilities in that comfortable home. It is here that "she found beauty, order, cleanliness and praise"; hence "more and more she neglected her house, her children, her man" (99). While we understand the causes of Pauline's confused priorities, her contemptuous treatment of her daughter may affect us no less powerfully than does Cholly's physical assault. And her later refusal to believe Pecola about the rape (together with her failure to prevent its recurrence) arguably puts both parents on a similar moral footing.

Morrison has written of *The Bluest Eye* that she "did not want to dehumanize the characters who trashed Pecola and contributed to her collapse" (foreword np). In the section focusing on Cholly's life and culminating in the rape, she constructs this character as a kind of unconventional tragic hero, as someone with whom we engage sympathetically without ever condoning. We learn that he was "abandoned on a junk heap by his mother, rejected for a crap game by his father" (*BE* 126), and that in his youth he was subjected to a grotesque ordeal by a group of white men who, stumbling on him in the midst of his first sexual encounter, with a local girl, Darlene, force him to continue it under their gaze. Given that this voyeurism is itself a kind of violation, the author sets Cholly's rape of his own daughter in a wider political context, insisting on the inevitable relatedness of racially and sexually motivated abuses of power. Morrison reinforces this point through the later account of Soaphead Church, whose inherited horror of "all that suggested Africa" translates into "a patronage of little girls"; paradoxically enough, his pedophilic tendencies are "associated in his own mind with cleanliness" and "smacked of innocence" (*BE* 132). By charting these men's passage through the corrupt and destructive cultures into which they are born, Morrison forces us to recognize that the ethics of sexual violence are both simple and complicated at once.

By describing the changing, contradictory emotions that Pecola's downtrodden demeanor provokes in Cholly, and by explaining that "the clear statement of her misery was an accusation" about his own unworthiness and shortcomings, the author puts us in the unsettling position of understanding a father's point of view as he rapes his own daughter (*BE* 127). We are made to see, despite our profound discomfort, that this character destroys Pecola at least in part out of his love for her. To acknowledge this point diminishes neither the enormity of Cholly's crime nor the extent of Pecola's suffering; it exemplifies the complexity of outrageous actions that all Morrison's novels explore.

The final and shortest section of the novel is "Summer." Besides the depiction of the two-voiced, psychotic Pecola, it comprises Claudia's account of the community's gossip about her friend, of the marigolds' failure to grow, of Cholly's death in the workhouse, and of Pecola's crazed ramblings around "that little brown house she and her mother moved to on the edge of town" (*BE* 162). A final quotation from the "Dick and Jane" reader, incomplete and without spacing or punctuation, precedes the dialogue between the bifurcated parts of Pecola's former self:

"LOOKLOOKHERECOMESAFRIENDTHEFRIENDWILLPLAYWITHJANETHEY WILLPLAYAGOODGAMEPLAYJANEPLA." (153)

This descent into disordered nonsense both anticipates Pecola's psychosis and represents the dismantling of the damaging value system that the novel sets out to subvert. Morrison has written of her self-conscious attempt to "hold the despising glance while sabotaging it"; she wants to depict racist narratives while depriving them of their power (*BE* foreword np). The Dick and Jane reader quite literally frames the story but is also quite literally broken up by it.

In the novel's closing pages, the tone becomes elegiac, and the mood unremittingly bleak: Pecola "spent her days, her tendril, sap-green days, walking up and down, up and down, her head jerking to the beat of a drummer so distant only she could hear" (*BE* 162). The adult Claudia realizes that the community's abnegation of their responsibilities to this peripheral child and their deterministic acceptance of her fate were "wrong," but that "among the garbage and the sunflowers of [her] town, it's much, much, much too late" (164). Morrison's phrase "my town" perhaps engages with the affirmative vision at the end of Thornton Wilder's Pulitzer Prize–winning play, *Our Town*. First performed in 1938, the piece depicts white American family life in New Hampshire, a purportedly universal representation that has little in common with black life in Lorain in the 1940s.

Critics are divided about just how negative the ending of this novel is. Pecola is unequivocally destroyed; as Claudia says, "The damage done was total" (*BE* 162). And, aside from the experiences of the central victim, the presence of characters such as Mr. Henry (the MacTeers' lodger, who molests Frieda) creates a picture of a threatening world in which all children are vulnerable to sexual and other violence. It is true that there is a spiritedness about Claudia that is never quashed despite all that she has witnessed, and that gives an enduring energy to her account. Moreover, in Morrison's depiction of the three prostitutes' kindness to Pecola, or in Mr. and Mrs. MacTeer's brusque but unconditional care for their daughters, the author affirms the values of love and protection. But the end of Claudia's prologue foreshadows the mood of the end of the novel itself: "Cholly Breedlove is dead; our innocence too. The seeds shrivelled and died; her baby too" (3). Morrison's first novel is very possibly her least optimistic in its closing vision.

Writing in 1993, Morrison observed that "the initial publication of *The Bluest Eye* was like Pecola's life: dismissed, trivialized, misread" (*BE* afterword 172). Speaking in Charleston in 2008 she said that in the late 1960s the novel was rejected twelve times before being accepted by a press. It is now, however, widely taught (often causing controversy) in schools and colleges across the world. Critics are in agreement about the depth and the sophistication of this short work and have explored many themes there is no space to expand on here, such as the resonances of World War II, the meaning of "home" in African-American experience, the ease with which a community scapegoats vulnerable individuals, or the strategic engagement with the classical myths of Demeter and Persephone, and of Tereus and Procne. Perhaps the greatest tribute to this novel, however, occurred in 2006. In Austria, in November of that year, the city of Vienna elected to distribute 100,000 free copies of *The Bluest Eye* (*Sehr Blauen Augen*) in its annual "One Town, One Book" event. Morrison was so gratified by the significance of this occasion, occurring sixty-one years after the death of Adolf Hitler, that she made sure she was present at its launch.

Sula (1973)

Sula is a spare, strange masterpiece. It focuses on a black community who live in "the Bottom," the hills above a fictional midwestern town called Medallion, through which the Ohio River runs. The action primarily takes place between 1919 and 1941 – from the end of World War I to the year of the U.S. entry into World War II. The final chapter is set in 1965 and depicts one of the two central protagonists, Nel, who is now aged fifty-five, reflecting with nostalgic grief on the past and on the nature and the loss of her friendship with the eponymous character, Sula.

Morrison's choice of *Sula* as title misleads the unsuspecting reader to brilliant effect. It plays on the expectation that those versed in a European literary tradition bring to the novel: that Sula must be the central character in a bildungsroman named for its primary focus on her. The author subverts this preconception by depicting a network of characters who all play key roles in the life of the Bottom: the shellshocked Shadrack; Eva and Hannah Peace (Sula's grandmother and mother); Nel Greene, her husband, Jude, and her mother, Helene Wright; Mr. Buckland Reed; the alcoholic Tar Baby; the mysterious trio of Deweys; and Sula's onetime lover, Ajax. While the book is certainly concerned with Sula's quest for fulfillment, this is by no means its only preoccupation. Through the counterpoint between the title's implications and the narrative that unfolds, Morrison enacts the complex relationship between individualism and communality that is one of her central concerns. The immediate challenge to European aesthetic convention is also very much to the point: the novel is replete with allusions to traditional West African culture and beliefs.

In a 2002 interview Morrison stated that *Sula* "talks about friendship between women at a time – I was writing it in 1969 – when women and women's subjects weren't considered worthy subjects for fiction" (*DC* 204). In the foreword she reiterates this primary theme, "What is friendship between women when unmediated by men?" (*S* xi), and explicitly connects the story with her own friendships with other women while living in New York City in 1969, a time of "snatching liberty" (*S* xiii, xv). But the novel treats countless other themes as well: motherhood; marriage and monogamy; female sexuality; self-knowledge, self-realization, and self-destruction; the relationship between the rational and the irrational, or order and disorder, or purity and impurity; the sterility of binary oppositions; the dangerous and paradoxical nature of freedom; the illogic inherent in the ideology of the American Dream; the ease with which a group scapegoats vulnerable individuals; the decline of community life in black neighborhoods; the persistence of pre- or counter-Enlightenment modes of thought and belief in African-American culture; the continued economic disenfranchisement of black people as the twentieth century progressed – these are just some of the issues that *Sula* explores.

The plot in itself involves an unexplained amputation, a mother's killing her son through burning him, her daughter's self-immolation, the drowning of a child, adultery, abandonment, and death by unexplained illness. Yet all is told in prose that is quiet, distilled, uncannily calm and poised. With the exception of one notable passage, *Sula* is related by a third-person fully omniscient narrative voice that recounts a broadly chronological sequence of events. This relatively simple narrative technique might lead you to expect a novel that is less complex than *The Bluest Eye*. Do not be deceived.

In "Unspeakable Things Unspoken," Morrison performs an illuminating close reading of *Sula*'s opening section. She highlights the significance of the opposition between the blackberries and the nightshade, of her attempt to encompass "the nostalgia, the history, the nostalgia for the history; the violence done to it and the consequences of that violence" (*UTU* 25).[1] "In that place," the novel begins, "... there was once a neighborhood" (*S* 3): here are conflict, change, and loss. Appropriating the elegiac tone we might associate with novelists such as Thomas Hardy or Willa Cather, Morrison depicts the ravaging effects of "progress" on a pastoral idyll in which lively children used to sit amid pear blossoms and on a vibrant cultural cohesiveness that is symbolized by the pool hall, the beauty parlor, and so on. The folkloric account of the origins of the Bottom – a white farmer's trick on his freed slave that the black community had turned to the good – itself exemplifies the kind of collective knowledge that would be decimated over time. In 1974, writing about *The Black Book*, Morrison articulates a perspective on retrospection that is highly relevant to *Sula*: "The point is not to soak in some warm bath of nostalgia about the good old days – *there were none!* – but to recognize and rescue those qualities of resistance, excellence and integrity that were so much a part of our past and so useful to us" (*WMM* 42; original italics). The prologue to *Sula* recognizes both those qualities and their loss, while the novel as a whole enacts a rescue of sorts.

The book's first of its eleven dated sections, "1919," explains how and why Shadrack has come to institute the bizarre and yet logical ritual of National Suicide Day. After his experience of World War I's trench warfare in France, his posttraumatic stress leaves him first straitjacketed in a psychiatric institution, and then discharged in a state defined by the absences or negatives that Morrison adeptly chronicles throughout her work: "no past, no language, no tribe, no source, no address book, no comb, no pencil, no clock," and so on (*S* 12). Detained overnight in a police cell he experiences an unglamorous but pivotal epiphany: he is reassured of his own reality, filled with joy by the "indisputable presence" of "blackness" when he confronts his own "grave black face" reflected in the toilet bowl (*S* 13).

On his return to the Bottom Shadrack assumes the role of neighborhood "crazy," simultaneously shunned and tolerated. Both the Suicide Day rite that he initiates (to make "a place for fear by controlling it") and the fact that the townsfolk come to "understand the boundaries and the nature of his madness" indicate a communal acceptance of the irrational that is antithetical to the rationalizing intolerance of Puritan-derived dominant American culture (*S* 14, 15). Shadrack implicitly functions as a West African priest figure or medicine man, and he and his ritual can be identified with specific divinities and traits in Vodun and Voudoun belief systems and practices.[2] His name, meanwhile, may allude to the Biblical Shadrach in Daniel (3.13–30), who refuses to worship a golden image set up by Nebuchadnezzar, is not burned by the flames of the furnace to which he is condemned, and so achieves a respect for his nonconformity and for the god to whom he has remained faithful. Morrison has described Shadrack (and his "organized, public madness") as a "disruptive remembering presence which helps ... to cement the community, until Sula challenges them" (*UTU* 27).

In the sections of the novel dated "1920" and "1921," Morrison creates the absolute juxtaposition between the Wright and Peace households, in the context of which the schoolgirls Nel and Sula become best friends. Helene Wright runs an immaculate home, and in the orderliness she imposes on Nel (which includes the pulling of her nose in order to "improve" it) she disowns the "funkiness" of her own childhood in New Orleans, where she was raised by her Catholic Creole grandmother, Cecile, while her mother, Rochelle, worked as a prostitute. The one-legged but magisterial Eva Peace, meanwhile, presides over an expansive "house of many rooms" (*S* 30), in which Hannah enjoys sex on a daily basis with various menfolk of the Bottom, and that provides a sanctuary for lost souls such as Tar Baby and the three Deweys. We learn of Helene and Nel's brief reverse migration from Ohio to New Orleans on the death of Cecile, a journey that the former finds deeply traumatic but that initiates the latter's realization of her own selfhood. We learn of Eva's abandonment by BoyBoy, and of her struggle and self-sacrifice (even of her own leg) to raise her children in the face of extreme poverty. Her later immolation of the drug-addicted Plum is the first of many outrageous acts in this novel that Morrison describes in minute detail but without explicit moral judgment, thereby challenging dominant conceptions of good and evil.

"1922" begins with a wonderful evocation of the burgeoning sexuality of Nel and Sula, now twelve years old. In the quiet but intense small-town atmosphere, walking to buy ice cream or back and forth from school, the girls notice and are noticed by the young (and underemployed) men, "the beautiful, beautiful boys" of the Bottom (*S* 56). Of their friendship, Morrison writes that "in the safe harbor of each other's company they could afford to abandon the ways of other people and concentrate on their own perception of things" (55). While many critics have emphasized the polar opposition of the two characters, Morrison's own comparison (in an interview) of the pair to a "a Janus' head" is important because it illuminates their complementariness, their power and completeness as a pair, as well as the conflict to which their different outlooks later give rise (*TG* 62). Their silent, companionate riverside play, in which their innocence is embodied in the purificatory burial of "small defiling things" (*S* 59), contrasts sharply with their undisclosed guilt about the accidental drowning of Chicken Little, who (witnessed only by Shadrack) slips out of Sula's arms as she spins him around. The fact that Sula walks right into Shadrack's shack, together with his vowing to keep her secret, establishes a connection between this pair. They share a lack of conformity to societal norms and are strongly identified with the nonrational, other-worldly occur-rences in the neighborhood. Morrison's detailed account of the restorative ecstatic grieving that Chicken Little's funeral involves is just one of the ways in which this novel works to counter a repressed and repressive version of white Anglo-Saxon Protestant (WASP) Christianity.

The year 1923 is one of troubling omens, painful conversations, and the dramatic denouement of Hannah's suicide by self-immolation, an act observed but not intervened in by Sula. Unlike the graphically described appearance of Hannah's burned body, the reason for her self-destruction is never made explicit. It is in this section, however, that we encounter the tripartite matriar-chal household of Eva-Hannah-Sula at its most dysfunctional. Echoing the trio of prostitutes in *The Bluest Eye* and anticipating similar paradigms in *Song of Solomon* and *Beloved*, it illustrates the danger of what Morrison has called "the absence of a constructive male presence" (*DC* 15). While Nel and Jude's lavish wedding at the end of part I suggests Nel's own desire for exactly that presence, her emasculated husband's expectation that "the two of them together would make one Jude" does not bode well for her future (*S* 83). Sula leaves town in the very middle of the book and on the very evening that Nel's marriage begins.

Part II begins ten years later, in 1937, with Sula's return to the Bottom. It is significant that we learn neither about the community during her absence, nor anything about her own experiences except that she had been "in college" and had had relationships with various men (*S* 99; 120). Nel is revitalized by her friend's return and rejoices in their shared laughter. Her subsequent dev-astation at finding Sula and Jude having sex, a double betrayal, strikes home because at this moment the narrative voice becomes a first-person monologue, addressed by Nel directly to Jude. Perhaps swayed by this emotive narrative form, readers of *Sula* commonly express their struggle to identify with Sula when she sleeps with Jude and are dismayed that Morrison's portrayal of her central character as a promiscuous woman appears to bolster rather than sub-vert a certain stereotype of black female sexuality. Arguably Sula's own ratio-nale, that she and Nel "had always shared the affection of other people" (*S* 119), is not persuasive; for many there is a sharp disparity here between Morrison's stated intentions and her narrative's effect. In 1976 Morrison spoke of her wish to make Nel a "warm, conventional woman" whose commitment to her quo-tidian duties makes her "magnificent" (*TG* 12–13), yet at this point in the novel she is indubitably more victim than hero. The epigraph to the novel, moreover, which is taken from Tennessee Williams's *The Rose Tattoo* (1951), a comic play about the sexually uninhibited nature of characters in a Gulf Coast Sicilian community, implies a humorous perspective on the female sexual appetite that is entirely missing from *Sula*. Yet the profoundly unsettling, unacceptable nature of Sula's behavior is surely exactly the author's point about her "outlaw" status, and about how she is judged by the communities both within and outside the text (*DC* 230).

Morrison introduces the section "1939" with an account of the ways in which the people of the Bottom demonize Sula. They treat her as a defiling presence, blame her for their misfortunes, and alienate her as some kind of witch (without actively persecuting her). Sula purportedly embodies evil when she puts Eva in an old people's home, sleeps with other women's husbands, or ("the unforgivable thing") sleeps with white men (*S* 112). In a non-European way of managing evil, however, the community "looked at [it] stony-eyed and let it run" (113). Sula's role – part witch, part scapegoat – paradoxically benefits the community, enabling them to "band together against the devil in their midst" (117–18). This irony reaches its logical conclusion in 1941, when the optimistic community, perceiving Sula's death to be good news, go on to experience freakish bad weather, a return to their old conflict-ridden ways, and the catastrophe of the collapsing tunnel. Morrison's depiction of that year's National Suicide Day march, one of miasmatic "curious disorder" of the "pied piper" parade (*S* 160; 158), contains elements both of carnival and of a frenzied ritual that is Dionysiac in its part-cathartic and part-destructive nature. Shadrack, unmoored by the death of Sula, presages with his bell the imminent doom of World War II and the Bottom's ensuing demise.

Between the parentheses of the community's judgments, Morrison presents an alternative view of Sula in a free indirect discourse in which the protagonist is closest to speaking for herself. Morrison develops a character who resists any unified, coherent trajectory and who lives an "experimental life" (*S* 118). Exposing the aporia at the heart of the American Dream, the author demonstrates that complete freedom such as Sula's involves freedom from ambition and from responsibility. Whether the character is commendably assertive and self-possessed or regrettably selfish and self-obsessed is a question that remains unanswered. "I want to make myself," Sula tells Eva (92); "I got my mind," she tells Nel; "I got me" (143). Desiring neither a family of her own nor economic self-sufficiency, she rejects both of the conventionally accepted routes available to women and yet fails to overcome the final cultural constraint of her gender, race, and class: that of artistic expression and fulfillment. "Like any artist with no art form," writes Morrison, "she became dangerous" (*S* 121). The author depicts her temporary sexual satisfaction with another free spirit, Ajax, and his departure, which is precipitated by her own uncharacteristic conversion to marriagelike behavior. Just as there is no single interpretation of the name "Sula,"[3] and just as the mark above her eye is variously perceived to be a "stemmed rose" and a "tadpole" (52; 59), the character encompasses a multiplicity that Morrison has described as a "complex, contradictory, evasive, independent, liquid modernity" (*UTU* 26).

While Sula presents a challenge to readers, she also challenges Nel. At their sickbed encounter of 1940 there is no tearful reconciliation. Instead, Sula asks Nel a question: "About who was good. How you know it was you?" (146). Rooted in the instability of the distinction between good and evil, and in the fraughtness of making moral judgments, this is a dilemma that Morrison's novels repeatedly pose. But it is not until 1965, when Eva challenges her about her role in the death of Chicken Little, that Nel allows herself to recollect Sula's death and lonely burial. The novel ends with her final realization that when she thought she had been missing Jude, she had really been missing her best friend. While some critics interpret her sorrowful cry, "girl, girl, girlgirlgirl" (174), as an expression of unfulfilled lesbian desire, the more commonly held view is that it articulates her pain at realizing the true value of a friendship destroyed so long ago. At its ending, therefore, *Sula* anticipates *Love* in its identification between nostalgia for the innocent intimacies of girlhood friendship and a complex sense of the losses that racial integration entailed for black Americans, alongside the gains.

Song of Solomon (1977)

In October 2008, shortly before being elected president, Barack Obama told a CBS News anchor that *Song of Solomon* was "one of [his] favorite books."[4] Obama is anything but alone in his admiration for this text: *Solomon* was published in 1977 to instant critical acclaim. The numerous awards and honors bestowed upon it both at that time and subsequently have established and maintained the stellar reputation of its creator.

In its focus on the life stories of a family named Dead, the novel functions on numerous levels simultaneously. It is the narrative of an individual's self-discovery, an examination of the way gender and class have shaped different versions of African-American experience, a rewriting of American history, and a dialogue with literary and cultural genealogies of American, African, and European provenance. Primarily spanning the decades from the 1930s to the 1960s, its action begins in a fictional lakeside city in Michigan, which makes it the third Morrisonian novel set in the Midwest. But its protagonist, the young man Milkman Dead (officially Macon Dead III), on whom the narrative predominantly focuses, sets out from his birthplace on a quest to find ancestral riches. As his search takes him first to rural Pennsylvania and then to rural Virginia, so the novel becomes at once epic and mock-epic in scope.

This is a novel about the black struggles for civil rights in the 1950s and 1960s, and about the violence and the intra- as well as interracial conflicts that those processes entailed. Its cinematic sweep also takes in the depression, black migration, the abuses of the Reconstruction era, and slavery itself. Defining both the work's historical reach and Milkman's quest is the folk memory of Solomon (also known as Shalimar), Milkman's great-grandfather, who flew back to Africa and gains legendary status in the children's rhyme to which the novel's title alludes. The quasi-myth of Solomon is just one example of the importance of African cultural practices, beliefs, and ways of knowing; this inheritance is also embodied in the character of Pilate, the sister (and antithesis) of Milkman's father, Macon Dead II. Milkman's discoveries about his father (a ruthless landlord, abusive husband, and authoritarian parent), his aunt (an unmaterialistic, infinitely loving woman endowed with special powers), and his ancestry as a whole, become a parable of sorts: about self-awareness and homecoming, and about the importance of African-Americans' uncovering and laying claim to their past.

Morrison consistently subverts her own parable-like narrative through her focus on the many failings and all-too-realistic foibles of her central characters. Demonstrating once again the inseparability of the personal and the political through the tyrannical Macon, the self-centered Milkman, and his sometime companion, the radical Guitar, Morrison explores patriarchy, the nature of male friendship, and the viability of a nonpatriarchal black masculinity in the struggle for civil rights. At the same time through Ruth Dead (Milkman's mother); I Corinthians and Magdalena (Milkman's sisters); Pilate's daughter, Reba; and Reba's daughter, Hagar, the author examines motherhood, siblinghood, and the nature of unfulfilled female ambition and sexual desire. Milkman's flight at the novel's ending – indeterminate in mood and ambiguous in meaning – epitomizes the unresolved tensions that its author begins to dramatize on its very first page. Morrison explores the relationship between heroism and anti-heroism, between the tragic and the comic, between myth and reality (or legend and history), between prophetic vision and the often-unpalatable wisdom of hindsight, and between triumph and defeat.

Michigan

The first and longer of *Song of Solomon*'s two parts opens with the somewhat mysterious account of a promise by one Robert Smith that, on an appointed day and time, he will "fly away on [his] own wings" (3). Smith's attempt at flight ends in a very public suicide, and its possible motive is not revealed until we learn from Guitar that this man was an erstwhile member of the violent activist group the Seven Days, who perpetrate retributive attacks in the name of "justice" against white murderers of blacks. It cannot be a coincidence, however, that the date of this character's ill-fated flight – "18th of February, 1931" [*sic*] is the birth date of Morrison herself (3). The fact that Milkman is born one day later, therefore, means that his age in relation to the historical events contextualizing his life exactly mirrors Morrison's own.

Equally significant in terms of the author's personal relationship to this novel must be its first dedication, "Daddy" (v), and her explicit assertion that this novel's "radical shift in imagination from a female locus to a male one" is attributable to the ways she was affected by the loss of her father, who died in 1975 (*SoS* x). "I can't tell you how I felt when my father died," she writes in "The Site of Memory" (1987), "but I was able to write *Song of Solomon* and imagine, not him, and not his specific interior life, but the world that he inhabited and the private or interior life of the people in it" (*WMM* 73). You may recall that the author's maternal grandfather (with whom she shared her childhood home) was named John Solomon Willis; this side of the family not only had Native American ancestry but were also subjected to unscrupulous dispossession from land in Alabama, in 1910.[5] *Song of Solomon*, then, exemplifies Morrison's own assertion that "the act of imagination is bound up with memory," but that at the same time "only the act of the imagination" can provide "total access to the unwritten interior life of these people" (*WMM* 71; 77).

From the outset, this novel draws our attention to its striking names, obliging us to decode and/or appreciate their significance. We encounter "Mercy" (a hospital as well as a recurring theme, for example, in Pilate's refrain at Hagar's funeral that anticipates *A Mercy*), "Not Doctor Street" (the black community's subversive label for Mains Avenue), and "Guitar" (which might as well be "Welsh" to the officious nurse who hears it (7)). Before we learn Milkman's official name (Macon Dead III), we discover that "Milkman" is a nickname given by the janitor, Freddie, who espies Ruth nursing him well past babyhood. By the end of the first chapter we are apprised of the invested nature of the naming process in the Dead family: Macon I was renamed thus by a "drunken Yankee" soldier who messed up his Freedman's Bureau registration form, while Pilate's "Christ-killing" name was chosen from the Bible by his father, who was illiterate but saw something "princely but protective" in those letters (18–19). While Macon II perceives a "monumental foolishness" in the way his family is named (15), Pilate carries the written form of her much-valued name in a box hanging from her ear.

The narrative sympathy in the novel as a whole endorses this character's belief in the importance of the act or the *process* of naming. In a world where "white people name Negroes like race horses" (243), as Guitar explains,

"Niggers get their names the way they get everything else – the best way they can" (88). Toward *Solomon*'s end, through Milkman's musings on the Greyhound bus, Morrison riffs fabulously on the storied and powerful nature of African-American names. She compiles an exuberant list of "names ... got from yearnings, gestures, flaws, events, mistakes, weakness. Names that bore witness" (331). As it was for Adam in the book of Genesis, to name something is to exert authority over it. The act of naming, therefore, is of supreme importance in the context of the African-American struggle for a viable identity, for power and rights that equal those of whites, and for the effective articulation of those struggles.

In the yearning of Milkman's father, Macon, for "some ancestor ... who had a name that was real" (*SoS* 17) lies a yearning for a heroic past or pedigree. As he grows into manhood Milkman looks for the same and seeks a heroic future for himself as well. Many critics have discussed Morrison's subversion of the conventions of both the bildungsroman and the epic genre through her protagonist's faltering and error-strewn search for identity and fulfilment. Her foreword is illuminating here: though she charts a conventional chronology in this book (following the story of Milkman's life from his birth to his death, sketching out the past only through characters' recollections rather than through direct depictions of different periods), the novel is "old-school heroic, but with other meanings" (*SoS* x). As numerous critics have observed, Morrison positions Milkman in a contrapuntal relationship to a range of archetypal heroes: the African-American escaped slave (who either flies back to Africa or creates a successful life in the free North), the American self-made hero epitomized in the novels of Horatio Alger, the wandering Homeric Odysseus or Ulysses (and all his subsequent literary configurations), the biblical Moses, and the tragic Oedipus, whose realizations about the truth of his life lead to his blindness and exile.

Milkman's path to enlightenment is not a process of steadily increasing revelation and self-knowledge, but rather a series of fits and starts, lapses and epiphanies. Each of his attempts to secure wealth and personal advancement results in a humiliating setback – he is arrested in his hometown, he ruins his clothes in the cave outside Danville, he is attacked in Shalimar – and his self-centered quest comes at an irreparable cost to his sisters, to Hagar, and to Pilate. In configuring this blundering, self-important but self-unseeing character, Morrison often deploys a free indirect discourse that gives us insights into the workings of his mind in a tone characterized by ironic, critical detachment. This contributes to readers' struggle to like or identify with Milkman, and in a further irony the glamorous and worldly-wise Guitar holds a much more instant appeal despite the violent crimes that he perpetrates. Morrison's ambivalent casting of her protagonist questions the nature of black masculinity, the relevance of the Western heroic tradition to the specificity of African-American experience, and dominant conceptions of heroism itself.

Morrison declared in a 1992 interview that in the scene where Milkman walks alone against the flow of the crowd she "used an Edvard Munch painting almost literally" (*WMM* 84). This painting is presumably *Evening on Karl Johan Street* of 1892, which in its juxtaposition of an isolated individual walking against a ghostlike crowd epitomizes a modernist sense of isolation and alienation. But Morrison is skeptical both about the ideology of individualism, a sacred tenet of dominant American culture, and about modernism's preoccupation with the angst-ridden self. Milkman's unforgettable line to Guitar after news of the death of Emmett Till (in 1955; see Chapter 2, "Other Creative Work"), "Fuck Till, I'm the one in trouble" (88), positions his existential angst in ironic relation to the political realities of the moment. The men's conversations in Tommy's Barbershop bear witness to decades of black exploitation and oppression – in both world wars, in the South, and ongoing in the North – about which Milkman is unashamedly unexercised. The author suggests that the protagonist's indifference to the nature of America's past and present is allied to his ignorance about his ancestry, and his political education begins with his piecemeal discoveries about the past experiences of Macon and Pilate. Through the backstories of Milkman's father and aunt, Morrison testifies to the necessity of what she calls, in her memorably entitled essay on the subject, "Rootedness: The Ancestor as Foundation" (1984).

It is hard for both Milkman and readers to believe that his outwardly successful, materially obsessed father is the brother of Pilate, whom the boy has been taught to regard as "ugly, dirty, poor, drunk" (*SoS* 36). In the second chapter, Milkman is privy to these characters' contrasting perspectives on a shared past, and on the contrasting trajectories to which that past has given rise. Macon's ruthlessness is partly explained by his experiences of working his father's land since he was "four or five," of witnessing both his father's self-made agricultural success and his murder at the hands of land-stealing whites (51). Pilate, by contrast, focuses on the people in her past: she recollects her mother, who died bearing her; her father, whose violent death she recalls in graphic detail; and Macon, who used to be the model of protective fraternal concern. The early scene in which the now-contemptuous Macon peers voyeuristically through the window at Pilate, Reba, and Hagar – at their singing, the atmosphere of spontaneity in their household, and Pilate's wine making – clarifies his role as the embodiment of a repressive rationality and his sister's as the embodiment of a nonrational, pre-Enlightenment spirituality. Mysteriously born with no navel, Pilate has a strikingly "African" face (54), is a "natural healer" (150), and practices traditional magic. She is receptive to beneficent visits by the spirit of her father, and as herself an ancestor figure she is fiercely protective of her family, even when this involves a performance of shape-shifting obsequiousness in order to secure the release from police custody of the treacherous Milkman and Guitar. Pilate also functions as a foil to Milkman: Morrison configures the account of her past with a notable absence of ironic detachment or authorial critical distance. Her wanderings and migrant labors with her geography book, told as one uninterrupted narrative, testify to her wit and resilience. The story of her life functions as the true heroic odyssey in the novel, against which Milkman and his deeply flawed stumblings are measured and fall almost comically short.

Morrison also devotes considerable attention to the lives of numerous other women in the text. Through Ruth Dead – devout daughter, unloved and oppressed wife, unrespected mother – the novel explores a simultaneous complicity in and resistance to abuse at male hands. Through Corinthians and Magdalena, meanwhile, Morrison dramatizes the economic reality that domestic work remained the only viable form of employment opportunity for many woman of color in the 1950s and 1960s, despite the promises that upward mobility and college education appeared to hold out. Milkman's unfounded contempt for the women in his family is trumped only by his shoddy treatment of his cousin and erstwhile-lover, Hagar. Through this young woman's crazed and violent response to the thank you letter by which he finishes his relationship with her, however, Morrison also rehearses one of the defining themes of her oeuvre: the folly and danger of excessive, self-surrendering passion.

Hagar, whose name recalls both Abraham's Egyptian concubine in Exodus and Pauline Hopkins's magazine novel *Hagar's Daughter* (1901–2), suffers from the absence of a "chorus of mamas, grandmamas, aunts, cousins, sisters" (*SoS* 307), and in her desire to own Milkman, to find in him her "home" (137), there is "something truly askew" (138). Her poignant death is genetically predestined, foreshadowed by the refusal to survive abandonment of her legendary great-grandmother, Ryna. But Morrison casts Hagar's passion in a critical light without diminishing either the serious exploration of frustrated female sexual desire or the exposure of the nonheroic, self-centered Milkman, whom, in 1963, an enraged Lena evicts from the family home.

Pennsylvania

The novel's second part begins by relating Milkman's adventures in Danville, Pennsylvania. In this tenth chapter Morrison achieves something of a paradox: she intensifies the archetypal nature of the narrative and, having set her protagonist apart from the competing cast of his Michigan hometown, simultaneously develops her analysis of his psyche. Milkman travels (by exhilarating airplane and debilitating Greyhound) to his father's birthplace in an attempt to "live [his] own life" (221–2), and to find the gold that he and Guitar had attempted to steal from Pilate's house, but that he now believes to be in a cave above her childhood home. He develops a blind hubris about his family and himself while enjoying the company of the Danville menfolk at Reverend Cooper's house. The community's collaborative memories conjure up his grandfather's farm at its zenith, one that "spoke to them like a sermon" about the viability of the American Dream (235). This defining encounter reenergizes the "clean-lined definite self" he had felt when planning the ill-fated theft with Guitar (184). Now, after a back and forth exemplifying Morrison's interest in the "call and response" form of black religious tradition (and the choric/protagonist relationship in classical drama), Milkman is giddy to be among those who knew his "people" (229) and basks hypocritically in their admiring recollections of his father and their delight in his own boasting.

Predictably, Milkman falls from his newfound height as soon as he encounters the hostile landscape that his grandfather had once tamed. When he arrives at the forbidding-looking Butler Place in search of Circe (the caretaker/midwife who had delivered Pilate and sheltered her and Macon after their father's death), he is disheveled and "a little anxious" (239). Morrison's description of this "dark, ruined, evil" building, with its decaying neoclassical facade, typifies the significance with which she invests architecture throughout her oeuvre (228). She also manipulates stereotype here: the violent, greedy, racist, and now-extinct Butler family epitomize characters usually associated with the Deep South, but Morrison sets this gothic history in purportedly enlightened Pennsylvania.

In comparing Milkman's approach to the house with Hansel and Gretel's, the author continues the self-conscious dialogue with the fairy tale genre that she initiates when comparing Ruth's illicit nursing to the gold-spinning miller's daughter. The analogy also leads us to expect that Circe is some kind of witch; when Milkman encounters the old "colorless" woman he assumes she "had to be dead" because she spoke with a young woman's voice (240). Surrounded by stinking dogs, she divulges crucial information, the name of his grandmother ("Sing") and her ethnicity ("Indian mostly" (243)); tells him that his murdered grandfather's real name was Jake; and gives him the directions to the cave where his body could be found.

Morrison's decision to name this mysterious but pivotal character "Circe" has provoked much critical discussion. Together with the author's labeling of the archetypal peripatetic African-American male "the Ulysses theme" in a 1976 interview (*TG* 26), the invocation of the Homeric Circe (who turns Odysseus's men into pigs and sends him to the underworld to question Tiresias) makes explicit the novel's relationship to the *Odyssey*. It also establishes a dialogue with Ralph Ellison's *Invisible Man*, which itself signifies importantly on the Greek epic. Yet, just as Milkman himself is at once like and significantly unlike the Sophoclean Oedipus (he has a slight limp; there is the hint of incest in his relationships with Ruth and Hagar), Morrison's Circe is unlike her Homeric predecessor in important ways. As Kimberly Benston has argued, Homer's Circe is one of the many women who function as obstacles to Odysseus's progress, whereas although Milkman is inexplicably aroused when he first encounters his Circe, she functions only to assist him on his path to enlightenment.[6] In depicting women as for the most part insightful, enabling presences in her novel, Morrison thus revises both Homer's and Ellison's deployment of bewitching or domestically smothering females. At the same time, however, the other-worldliness of Morrison's Circe is significant for different and politically specific reasons: the character epitomizes the "sacred ritual specialist" of Western and Central African tradition.[7] Her presence thus testifies to the interrelatedness of classical and African cultures, which is a key preoccupation of Morrison's work as a whole and which is reiterated in the Shalimar children's song.

Shalimar, Virginia; Back to Michigan; Back to Virginia Again

"The women's hands were empty" (*SoS* 259): through that single but inspired detail, Morrison conveys the material poverty of Shalimar, Virginia. The fiasco of the gold's nondiscovery in the cave must have become remote, because Milkman's behavior on arrival in the one-store town of his forebears suggests that he has learned little in the way of humility. Momentarily unnerved by Guitar's cryptic message that his "day was coming" (263), his insensitive parading of his wealth and "Northernness" lands him in a fight with local young men. Morrison exposes her character's self-importance and self-pity through an ironic echo of Mark's Gospel (4.5): "Here, in his 'home', he was unknown, unloved, and damn near killed" (*SoS* 270).

The bobcat hunt with the older Shalimar menfolk functions as a quasi-mythical test for Milkman; it is an initiation rite into southern manhood. At its end he feels a new kind of belonging, as though his legs were rooted trees, "and he did not limp" (281). As John Duvall has argued, this scene comprises an important dialogue with Faulkner's story sequence, *Go Down, Moses* (1942); Morrison revises the earlier novelist's sense of patrimonial, predestined doom.[8] Yet although the detailed portrayal of the physically exhausted

Milkman's "stream of consciousness" reveals that he has acquired insight into the errors of his previous ways, Morrison still does not grant him unqualified heroic status. At the very moment that he believes he "understood Guitar now" (*SoS* 278), his former friend surprises him with razor wire around the neck. Milkman only escapes by firing his gun, and while he watches the men butcher the dead animal, he recalls the past conversations in which Guitar attempted to justify the violence of the Seven Days.

Guitar's subsequent two reappearances – on the road after Milkman's visit to Susan Byrd's and in the woods at the novel's denouement – convey a sense of his descent into a psychotic bloodthirstiness. Five years earlier there was a brutal logic behind the militants' attacks on randomly selected whites: "Numbers. Balance. Ratio" (158). This Florida-born character's account of the failure of the law courts to bring racist whites to justice is compellingly true (155). His rhetoric of polluting blood and retributive direct action, which articulates the more radical end of the black activist spectrum and recalls both traditional West African penal practices and the discourse of crime and vengeance in the *Oresteia*, is chilling but comprehensible. But Guitar's conviction that white people are biologically depraved, "in their blood, in the structure of their chromosomes" (157), contrasts sharply with Pilate's insights about the arbitrariness of racial categorization – "black ... moves and changes from one kind of black to another" (41) – and his motive for trying to kill Milkman is based on his misconception that the younger man had found and secreted the gold. Morrison – for whom "counter-racism was never an option" (*H* 4) – documents the way that Guitar's "eye for an eye" ideology ultimately renders him "crazy" (*SoS* 295).

Milkman is able to complete his genealogy through two conversations with Susan Byrd (his newly discovered cousin) and through hearing the words of the children's singing game, "Jake the only son of Solomon" (303). Susan tells him that Solomon one day "flew back to Africa," leaving behind his wife, Ryna, and dropping his son, Jake (322). Jake was brought up by Heddy, mother of Sing, with whom he later made the journey to Pennsylvania. It is difficult to overemphasize the importance of the Solomon song in this novel or to Morrison's project as a whole. The fact that Pilate sings one version of it, ("O Sugarman"), on the novel's sixth page and before Milkman's birth (6), while the children play it as a "ring-around-the-rosy" in 1963 (264), testifies to two fundamental aspects of African-American dynamism: the strength of the oral tradition as a means of cultural transmission and of folk memory as (coded) knowledge. Moreover, every word and line in the song bears close analysis.[9] The song's hybridized nature testifies to the complexity of African-American identity and illustrates Morrison's argument (discussed in Chapter 3, "Transnationalism,

Modernism and Postmodernism") that the dislocations and reconfigurations of modernism are epitomized by the American South. While critics have interpreted the author's engagement with the cultural memory of flying Africans as an upbeat and emancipatory gesture, we should not fail to note the authorial ambivalence about the flying paradigm. Scholars detect resonances of Icarus and of James Joyce's Stephen Dedalus, and implicit in the trope is a critique of self-centered male departure and ascent. The abandoned Ryna, whose devastated wailing still echoes in the woods, anticipates the irreparable grief of the abandoned Hagar. Without diminishing her condemnation of those prone to excessive, self-negating passion, Morrison also subjects to scrutiny the black male's individualistic flight through various means: through moments of comic realism, such as Susan's observation about the strain of being a single parent; through playing on Ovid's myth of Echo and Narcissus to suggest the narcissism of Solomon and of Milkman; and through the montage technique of chapters 12–14, in which she alternates between an ever-more-euphoric traveling Milkman and a defeated-then-dead homebound Hagar. Indeed, Hagar's miserable demise and poignant funeral function as a counternarrative to the biblical Song of Solomon (or Song of Songs), in which a "black, but comely" woman and a man express the perfection of their mutual love (Song of Songs 1.4).

In the novel's final chapter, Morrison exploits the irony that while her male protagonists believe "everybody wants a black man's life" (*SoS* 331), the unambiguous pathos lies instead in the deaths of two women. Milkman has no inkling of Hagar's fate until Pilate transforms his anticipated triumphant homecoming into a below ground penance. The description of the old woman's being shot by Guitar, after burying her father's bones on Solomon's Leap, is understated to the point that we are shocked when we realize she is dying. Whether Milkman's own last-page leap will culminate in his flying, his suicide, his murder of or his murder by Guitar, we can never ascertain for sure.

Tar Baby (1981)

Tar Baby is set primarily outside the United States. Its principal location is a fictional small Caribbean island called Isle des Chevaliers, which translates (with significant ambiguity) as "the island of horsemen, cavaliers, or knights." This island is situated close to a second, larger one: Dominique. Dominique is also fictional, but its name's important connotations include the contemporary Dominican Republic; the neighboring country on the same Greater Antillean island, Haiti (which when a French colony was known as Saint-Domingue);

and the leader of the Haitian Revolution/slave rebellion beginning in 1791, whose full name was François Dominique Toussaint L'Overture.

The novel is set it in the years 1979–80, contemporaneous with the time in which it was written.[10] While both global history and the characters' past experiences are crucial to the novel's present, the story of the septuagenarian millionaire Valerian Street and his wife, Margaret, runs only from before Christmas one year to the following fall. While the mansion-dwelling Streets, he a former candy magnate from Philadelphia and she his trophy wife from Maine, are the first white people to be fully realized individual characters in Morrison's fiction, nonwhite characters are of equal importance in the text. These include their cook and butler, Ondine and Sydney Childs, and the Childs's niece, Jadine (all black American); the intruder-turned-house-guest, Son (also black American); and the casual domestic "help," Gideon, Marie Thérèse, and Alma Estée (born on Dominique of African descent).

The Caribbean island setting enables Morrison to explore the relationships between race, class and power (at once complex and all too simple) in the interactions of these three different sets of people. The location also functions as a microcosm of the history of the Americas: both in bringing to mind Columbus's "discovery" of Hispaniola (the island that now comprises the Dominican Republic and Haiti) and as both the final destination for some enslaved Africans and a point of sale to North American slave dealers for others. As I discuss at more length in Chapter 3, Jadine's past life as a student and fashion model in Paris, combined with the Caribbean focus and the brief scenes in New York and Florida, positions the United States in a relative, transnational context in this novel – one that undermines its conventional exceptional status.

There are two separate but connected central plots in *Tar Baby*. The first concerns the Streets' marriage, which is apparently in a state of terminal decline when the novel opens. The relationship is further damaged by Margaret's fury at Valerian's inexplicable hospitality to Son and reaches a crisis when Ondine speaks out about Margaret's physical abuse of her and Valerian's own son, Michael. Meanwhile, the sophisticated and pale-skinned Jadine (whose education Valerian has sponsored) embarks on a passionate affair with the uncouth, dark-skinned, outlaw Son. They flee the island for New York, but their incompatible political and cultural perspectives (which are exacerbated by a visit to Son's Florida hometown, Eloe) lead to mutual contempt, blazing rows, physical attacks, and sexual violence by Son.

Through the orphan Jadine, Morrison explores the dangers of cultural orphanhood: in her commitment to conventional success, Jadine has dissociated herself from the African elements of her past. She believes that Western art is superior to African and ignores African-American spiritual and family traditions and obligations. She is deaf to ancestral wisdom and, in Thérèse's view, has "forgotten her ancient properties" (305). In these words spoken on the penultimate page of the novel, Morrison echoes the dedication on its first, which is to her aunts, her maternal grandmother, her mother, her sister, "and each of their sisters, all of whom knew their true and ancient properties" (np). We might readily assume that the way the book's end recalls its dedication imbues the text with a morally didactic message, an encouragement to side with Thérèse and Son against Jadine. Yet the novel's subsequent epigraph prepares us for apparently infinite ethical complexity, for the profound conflicts and moral ambiguity of the drama that enfolds.

"It hath been declared ... by them which are of the house of Chloe, that there are contentions among you," reads the epigraphic quotation from St. Paul's first letter to the Corinthians (np). To recall that Morrison's name at birth was Chloe Wofford is to understand that the "house of Chloe," on one level, refers to her own family: her family has told her that there are "contentions" among her "brethren." This speaks to Morrison's central concern in the novel: to explore and deplore the ideological clashes, the mutual misunderstandings, and the acts of intraracial violence and betrayal that have – for many, complicated, and understandable reasons – characterized the African diaspora since the inception of the transatlantic slave trade. In this sense the book is a logical successor to the three novels that precede it, each of which is similarly centered on conflicts within African-American communities. Morrison's testimony to her grandmother in the 2004 foreword suggests that what she has inherited from her family ultimately endorses rather than diminishes that sense of complexity, that interest in conflicting ideology. As the foreword recounts, one of Morrison's principal memories of her grandmother is of her telling stories, in particular the "puzzling" Tar Baby tale (*TB* xiii).

The Tar Baby tale is one of two narratives that underpin the stories that *Tar Baby* tells; the other is that of the blind horsemen from whom the Isle des Chevaliers derives its name. The former is part of African-American oral folkloric tradition and is rooted in West African trickster tales. Though there are many versions of the story, the predominant account is that there was once a farmer (or in Joel Chandler Harris's account of "the wonderful Tar-Baby story," Brer Fox) who entrapped a cabbage-stealing rabbit on a sticky black "contrapshun," but then unwittingly returned him to his favorite milieu, the briar patch. The most obvious reading of the novel in terms of this fable is to understand Valerian as the farmer, Jadine as the "tar baby side-of-the-road whore trap" (*TB* 220), and Son as the cunning rabbit who runs "lickety split" into his own briar patch, the island hills, on the novel's final page (306). Yet, as Morrison attests, "the story begged and offered understanding beyond 'outlaw peasant outwits inventive master with wit and cunning'" (*TB* xii). Both Son and the female spirits inhabiting the trees on the swamp in their turn entrap Jadine; the unmodernized African-American and the African past have elements of dangerous tar about them just as Jadine does.

The legend (or cultural memory) of the blind horsemen is similarly ambiguous in what it teaches. As Thérèse relates to Son, the horsemen are the spirits or descendants of slaves who, together with their enslaving French crew, became blind when they first saw Dominique (152). Yet Valerian understands the island's name to connote imperial power: "one hundred French chevaliers" enjoying "the security of the Napoleonic Code" (206). Despite Thérèse's unambiguous encouragement, in Morrison's own opinion (in 1981) it is possible to view Son's choice to "join these men" as an act of self-imprisonment rather than of liberation (*TG* 111). "He would lock himself up forever from the future," she has said. "He may identify totally and exclusively with the past, which is a kind of death" (*TG* 112). When Son, about to jump off the boat, asks Thérèse, "Are you sure?," it is no surprise that "if she answered, he could not hear it" (*TB* 306). *Tar Baby* and the stories that resonate in it dramatize brilliantly the "contentions" of the American 1980s – but they certainly provide no solutions.

Towards the end of the novel, Sydney observes of the mansion's disrepair, "This place dislocates everything" (84). Morrison anthropomorphizes the natural world of the island, and depicts the house itself as a near-living entity, in order to convey the many violations that the white colonizers have wrought. Following the prologue that narrates Son's furtive swimming ashore, the first of the novel's ten chapters begins with a description of the destruction of the previously Edenic environment that "laborers" have been "imported from Haiti" to bring about (9). The opening paragraph reads as a rewriting or reversal of various myths of creation – in the book of Genesis, for example, in John Milton's *Paradise Lost*, and in Ovid's *Metamorphoses*. The author writes a myth of destruction, in which the Sein de Vieilles, or "witch's tit," uncompromisingly subverts F. Scott Fitzgerald's iconic image of the "fresh green breast of the new world" at the end of *The Great Gatsby* (1926). She thereby deromanticizes the entire history of European conquest and settlement of the Americas.

The ironies of the mansion's name, "L'Arbe de la Croix," appear to be lost on Valerian. The "tree of the cross" connotes both the crucifixion of Jesus and the symbol of the Kongo Yowa, the cross within the circle that West Africans transported to the Americas, often retained in their religious belief and practice, and that is particularly important in Haitian Voudoun (or Voodoo).[11] Morrison also borrows the convention of the chorus (a feature of both Greek and West African drama) to imbue the Fog, the angel trumpet flowers, and the avocado trees with a commentating role. She then introduces the reader to the members of the household in near-cinematic fashion: at any one moment, she zooms in on each individual or grouping in turn. Occasionally (when every character is in bed, for example) we feel as though we are looking inside a doll's house, observing connected and conflicting lives being simultaneously lived in different spaces.

We first encounter Valerian at his breakfast table, fussing and being fussed over by Sydney. "Named after an emperor" (146), he has a sense of entitlement and arrogant imperiousness that are soon apparent. His self-satisfied contempt for those around him is demonstrated by his indifferent laziness about their names, and Morrison emphasizes this through her strategy of deferring the revelation of those names. We first encounter Margaret, for example, as "the Principal Beauty of Maine" (11). In his complacency, epitomized by the firing of Gideon and Thérèse for the theft of some apples, Valerian embodies the centuries of white exploitation that drove slavery and the colonial enterprise and that continue to drive its legacies. His family's business – candy – would historically have depended on the slave-produced sugar of the Caribbean, and (as in *Solomon*) there is a miasmatic quality to sweet foods in this novel. Readers identify with Son's intense fury at the Christmas table, both in his interior monologue about imperialist greed and waste, and in his provocative confrontations with his host. Yet Morrison complicates the morality of her tale by exploring in empathetic detail Valerian's grief about Michael's suffering and his remorse that he was "innocent" of it (243). Likewise, while Margaret is clearly stupid, overindulged, vain, and racist, Morrison encourages readers to identify with her sense of bewilderment, of "feeling drowned" at having to play the role of Valerian's wife after her impoverished Italian-American upbringing, in which her beauty was already an isolating burden (58). Morrison portrays Margaret's guilty recollections of her abusive behavior in ways that make us understand her actions without condoning them. At the novel's end, Valerian is a pathetic figure and Margaret has the newfound energy of the shriven. The couple undergo a reunion of sorts.

In her final chapter, Morrison implies that a reversal of the power dynamic between the Streets and Sydney and Ondine is taking place. Drinking Valerian's wine in front of him, the butler quietly makes it plain that he is now in charge. For the majority of the novel, however, these servants are alternately insulted, unsettled, and enraged by the events that unfold. Sydney dreams of his birthplace, Baltimore, whence he moved to Philadelphia; the couple have now served Valerian for fifty-one years. Their strong sense of propriety is easily offended by the many disruptions to the conventional order of the household (such as

Margaret's ill-fated decision to cook the Christmas meal). Their position in relation to racial politics is complex: Ondine is content to call Gideon "Yardman"
(161), and the pair's outrage at Valerian's indulgence of Son is based in part
on Sydney's perception of the latter as a "wife-raper" and a "stinking ignorant
swamp nigger" (99, 100). They take pride in their status as skilled and industrious
"Philadelphia Negroes" (63). Sydney is aware of "the book of that name," published in 1899 by W. E. B. Du Bois (284), and they look down on the black people
of the islands. They are not safe from racism themselves, however: Margaret,
Ondine's former companion, turns on her in an attempt to prevent the revelations about the abuse: "Shut up! You nigger! You nigger bitch!" (208).

Sydney and Ondine's sense that Jadine betrays them is profound. The
daughter of Sydney's brother, Jadine was raised by them as their own when
she became an orphan, and they paid her living costs at college, waited on her
as she sat with Valerian at the dinner table, and for a while "looked to her for
solutions to their problems" (91). After the Christmas debacle, they can never
reconcile themselves to the fact that she "ran off" with "that thing" (283), and
Ondine's suspicion that Jadine only returned to the island to fetch her sealskin
coat is probably justified. The aunt reproaches herself for never having passed
on important moral information that a daughter needs to know, but her and
Sydney's pain at their realization they will have to "bury [them]selves" persists
(284). They remain dignified to the novel's end but are profoundly isolated by
the multiple displacements they have undergone.

When we encounter Son in the novel's prologue, jumping from a U.S. naval
ship and then swimming to stow away on a private yacht, we know neither
his name, his location, nor his history. We are told only that "he believed he
was safe" (3); we learn that he is hungry but resilient and resourceful. While
the Middle Passage resonates in this novel's beginning and ending at sea,
Son's survival of a vortex and treacherous currents "like the hand of an insis-
tent woman" gives him a mythical quality from the outset (4). When we next
encounter him, however, some seventy pages later, Morrison discloses his
racial identity through describing him from the white subject position that has
until now prevailed at L'Arbe de la Croix: Sydney directs into the dining room
at gunpoint "a black man with dreadlock hair" (80). Having discovered him in
her closet, Margaret immediately assumes that Son intended to rape her, and
her anxiety that his "black sperm" would soil her designer wardrobe reaches
near-comic proportions (86).

Jadine is both concerned that the intruder poses a sexual threat and dis-
concerted to find him attractive. Morrison uses a recurring image of "small
dark dogs" to express Jade's desire for the uninvited guest (94; 113; 115). The
girl is thrown into confusion by his intrusion into her bedroom, his desire for

her, and his interest in her modeling career as "the copper Venus" (113); and by his contempt for her political outlook. He is equally disarmed by his own attraction to her. Both characters resort to stereotypical assumptions about the other: he asks her, "Why you little white girls think somebody's trying to rape you?" (120), while she calls him an "ape" and is overwhelmed by what she calls his "Mau-Mau, Attica, chain-gang hair" (113). We are privy to Jade's furious thoughts after he has "pressed his loins" into her and comments on her "smell" (122). Through Jadine's life story Morrison revisits and revises the trope of the "tragic mulatto," engaging particularly with the pale-skinned Helga Crane in Nella Larsen's 1928 novel *Quicksand*. We have already learned of her discomfort with her racial self-positioning, epitomized by her memory of the tar-skinned "African woman" in the yellow dress and headscarf in a Parisian supermarket (*TB* 45–6). She has come to the island to try to decide whether or not to marry the Paris-based white man Ryk, who she fears only wants her for the exotic blackness he believes she represents (48). Now, after her encounter in the bedroom with Son, she gets over any discomfort about "telling on a black man to a white man," resolves to have Valerian "haul the 'nigger' away" (126), and plans an escape to Miami with Margaret.

At this point, nearly midway through the novel, we still know very little about Son, and we do not yet know his name. As he takes a long shower (one of many symbolic acts of cleansing in the text), we are privy to his thoughts about how he survived in the mansion until now. We learn that he had been "running" for eight years under "seven documented identities," and finally we learn that "the name that called forth the true him" is "Son" (139). This name both suggests that Son is a kind of Everyman and plays on Valerian's lack of knowledge of his own son, Michael. After his apology to Sydney and Ondine, a short-lived pre-Christmas calm descends on everyone in the household except him: lying sleepless in a hammock he meditates on his status "without human rites," his obsession with Jadine, and his perception of the United States as "slick with the blood of all the best people" (167).

Given the narrative preeminence of the relationships between Valerian and Margaret, and between Jadine and Son, readers commonly overlook the significance of Gideon, Thérèse, and Alma Estée on first reading, thereby sidelining them exactly as the dominant culture does. But close analysis reveals that the novel is replete with details about their past and present that are central to Morrison's political project. A key point is that Son and these three Caribbean blacks have a relationship that exists independently of the Childs and the Streets. Gideon and Thérèse are aware of Son's presence days before anyone else, and they facilitate his access to food; Son, meanwhile, is profoundly moved by the hardships that "the old man's spine" embodies (139). We learn that Thérèse is Gideon's aunt, is "damn-near blind" (107), is a possible descendant of the blinded slaves in the "fishermen's tale" Gideon recounts to Son (152), and speaks "the French of Dominique" better than she speaks English, and that her breasts still lactate. She had "tricked" Gideon into returning from the "humiliations" of his immigrant life in the United States (111). She never looks at white people, believes they feel nothing at all, and refuses to speak to Sydney and Ondine.

Gideon and Thérèse maintain a state of slow but steady rebellion against their employers. Both conduct their tasks with a deliberately vengeful sloppiness, and in the tradition of the rebellious slave they hide their literacy from their employers (154). Despite their critical perspective on the United States, however, they "parade" Son around Queen of France "like a king" (149), succumb to his perceived glamour (Alma Estée begs him for a wig), indulge him in their home, and enable him to return to the United States with Gideon's passport. The many paradoxes of their lives and situation epitomize the complex and conflicted nature of black experience in the Caribbean as a whole.

The relationship between Jadine and Son becomes closer on their picnic excursion, but to the reader this same outing accentuates the differences between them. With obvious symbolism, Morrison follows the picnic with the pivotal episode in which Jadine attempts to draw a ring of trees, falls into the swamp, and is observed by the female tree spirits. These spirits represent the "sacred properties" of an essential and original Mother Africa, and the stinging, cloying "moss-covered jelly" (182), described variously as "oil," "mud," and "pitch" (184–5), represents the black past from which Jadine has spent her life trying to escape. While Morrison stages the near-drowning of Jadine in black mud as her intimacy with Son increases, Son views their escape to New York City as his "rescue" of Jade's mind and body from "the plantation" (219). The prose describing the happy days of their intense romance in this city is energized in a way that anticipates *Jazz*. Yet the exuberant confidences the couple exchange – about her mother's funeral or his experience of the war in Vietnam – is punctured by the refrain "He insisted on Eloe" (223–5; 228). Morrison's observation that they leave for small-town Florida "hand-in-hand" continues the Miltonic theme from the stolen apples of Christmas dinner (230); in its echo of Adam and Eve's expulsion from paradise at the end of *Paradise Lost*, it presages the end of the couple's happiness.

The brief stay in Eloe is the catalyst to the demise of the pair's relationship because it exacerbates their difference: Son fits right back in to his old hometown, while Jade is made to feel at first marginal, and then immoral. She is terrified by a dream of all the women she has ever known baring their breasts – a dream that challenges her authenticity as a black woman. The increasingly violent rows begin when Son returns to New York. Here, after Jade slaps and bites

Son, he holds Jadine out of the (high-up) window by her wrists, recalling Clare Kendry's death in Larsen's *Passing*. "This rescue was not going well," recounts Morrison. "One had a past, the other a future, and each one bore the culture to save the race in his hands" (269). When Son suddenly rapes Jade, the way Morrison describes the event makes it one often missed by readers. Just as the reciprocal lovemaking had been conveyed through the language of the throbbing star, now Morrison conveys Son's violent attack through his narration of a version of the Tar Baby story. The rhythm of his speech – (about the "bullshit bullshit bullshit farm") – mirrors the rhythm of the rape (270). The scene is as shocking as any in the Morrisonian oeuvre, in part because the author has already subverted characters' and readers' prejudiced assumption that a black man hiding in a closet must be intent on committing rape. The "slippery, gutted" Jadine leaves him for good (271).[12]

Morrison maintains indefinitely the conflict between the positions that Jade and Son hold. There is little to admire about Jadine as she leaves Dominique for Paris: she has renounced her filial duties to Sydney and Ondine, and when she finally recognizes Alma Estée, who now cleans the airport toilets, she refers to her offhandedly as "Mary" (290). Yet there is much that she has spoken during her arguments with Son that we cannot dismiss as "wrong." She points out, for example, that Valerian paid for her education when "nobody else did" (263). Immediately after the rape she speaks what may be her wisest words: "There is nothing any of us can do about the past but make our own lives better ... that is the only revenge" (271). As the plane takes off, she realizes that she herself "was the safety she longed for" (290).

Son's future, as set up by the novel's epilogue, is even more uncertain than Jadine's. He flees in the opposite direction from Jadine, at Thérèse's behest, to the island hills. Is this destination his briar patch? Is it an environment in which he will flourish or perish? Morrison writes in the foreword of her great-grandmother, her grandmother, her mother, and herself "peopling the writing of *Tar Baby'* as "witness, as challenge, as judges" (xiv). This discourse of the legal system is to the point: as readers we identify with both Son and Jadine, and we are unlikely to fulfill the "beseeching" of St. Paul in I Corinthians, to be "perfectly joined together ... in the same judgement" (I Corinthians 1:10). We are left confronting both the need and the impossibility of judging the right and the wrong in this case.

Beloved (1987)

Beloved is a book that gets under your skin. It is Morrison's best-known work, and like all of her novels, it is many things at once. It is an exploration of the experience of slavery and its aftermath from the perspective of those who were enslaved. It is an investigation of the nature of love and of the ways that love, in all its forms, is shaped by and shapes particular historical circumstances. It is a book about memory, both individual and collective or cultural. It is a ghost story. And it is also a brilliantly successful experiment in narrative form.

The novel tells the story of Sethe, a young former slave woman living on the outskirts of Cincinnati, Ohio, who in 1873 is visited by the ghost of Beloved. Beloved is (or was) the daughter whom she had killed as a baby eighteen years earlier, a month after her escape from the Kentucky plantation (Sweet Home) and on the point of her family's recapture into slavery. This is a tale that demands the complexity of the techniques through which Morrison tells it: multiple narrative voices, a disrupted chronology, a piecemeal revelation of events. It is a novel that richly rewards slow, careful reading and rereading. It asks that we be attentive to its densely woven allusiveness to a range of literary, musical, and religious traditions. Morrison here listens and gives voice to those whom the novel's epilogue calls "the disremembered and unaccounted for" (323): *Beloved* is a rewriting of defining chapters in American history, a reimagining that fulfills the author's stated imperative that "the past has to be revised" (*TG* 264).

The foremost concept in *Beloved* is a term Morrison coins within the novel itself: "rememory." The author uses the word as both noun (43) and verb, for example, in Sethe's asking Beloved, "You rememory me?" (255). When we first encounter Sethe she struggles to escape her memories and devotes considerable energy to "beating back the past" (85). The appearance of the ghostly Beloved forces her to confront that past, and eventually to 're-remember', or "re-member" (in the sense of reassemble) or to "re-memory" it, and this facing up to her traumatic experiences is key to her exorcizing them and moving forward. The process Sethe undergoes has much in common with conventional psychotherapeutic practice; at the same time there are here strong resonances of the Roman Catholic idea of shrivening, and of the general Christian idea of a baptism that enables a rebirth or a new beginning. In giving voice to "the black and angry dead," whom Stamp Paid hears "roaring" around Sethe and Denver's home (234; 213), the text also articulates a collective desire for vengeance and enacts a process of atonement for a whole people.

A second unifying premise is that the experiences of both Sethe and her community at large have remained both "unspeakable" and "unspoken" until now (235). The novel articulates the stories of many: of Sethe's horribly brutalized mother who survived the Middle Passage, of Sixo (a Sweet Home escapee who was burned to death as punishment), and of Paul D (another former Sweet Home slave, who, having survived a traumatic past, now becomes Sethe's lover). Through the relation of these details as much as through the telling of its central action – the murder of a baby, an act of infanticide by a mother – *Beloved* speaks the unspeakable at last.

In "The Site of Memory," Morrison describes "the matrix" of her work as "the wish to extend, fill in and complement slave autobiographical narratives" (*WMM* 77). She talks particularly of the silence, in those texts, about the individuals' "interior life" (*WMM* 70). *Beloved* is noteworthy, by contrast, for its fully developed explorations of the psychology of its characters. We become intimately acquainted with the thoughts of Denver (Sethe's surviving but alienated younger daughter), of Baby Suggs (Sethe's mother-in-law, the now-bedridden former preacher), and of Stamp Paid, the elderly "agent, fisherman, boatman, tracker, savior, spy," who helped escaping slaves cross the Ohio River from the slave state Kentucky to the free state Ohio (160). We are shown the workings of Sethe's mind so that we understand the fraughtness of her tragic dilemma: whether to allow her children's return to slavery or to end their lives herself and so to "put [them] where they'd be safe" (193). Like Baby Suggs, we can "not approve or condemn [her] rough choice" (212). The way that Morrison combines the psychology of individuals with wide-reaching political and historical interventions is one of the most striking aspects of her work, and never more so than in *Beloved*.

In "Rediscovering Black History" (1974) and in the foreword to this novel, the author attests to the formative experience of compiling the documentary history *The Black Book*. It was while working on that project that she came across the story that became her starting point for *Beloved*: a clipping from the *American Baptist* newspaper of February 1856 in which one Reverend P. S. Bassett describes his visit with an imprisoned slave woman, Margaret Garner, and reports her account of killing her child on the point of recapture into slavery (*BB* 10). *The Black Book* documents slavery in numerous ways, and Morrison's profound knowledge of the system that enslaved her own great-grandparents resonates in the broad epic sweep of the novel. In its three numbered parts that are divided into shorter sections of varying length, *Beloved*'s geographical scope ranges from Ohio and Kentucky through Texas and the Deep South to New York State and includes the Middle Passage. Its eye for sociological complexity incorporates the interaction between the Cherokees and Paul D, and the contrasting political perspectives between different white people such as Mr. Bodwin, the Garners, and the schoolteacher. Its emotional range encompasses agony, resilience, love in all its forms, and humor.

Part I

The novel opens in 1873, and its "present" spans the time from 1873 until the exorcism of Beloved in 1874. Morrison intends her opening description of the haunted 124 Bluestone Road to be "excessively demanding," one in which "the reader is snatched, yanked, thrown into an environment completely foreign" (*UTU* 32). Through this first depiction of the house where Sethe, now thirty-seven, lives with Denver, now eighteen, we also discover much about the household's past. We learn that Sethe's older two children, her sons Howard and Buglar, had run away from the machinations of the occupying baby ghost nearly a decade earlier, and that Baby Suggs, their paternal grandmother, had died soon after that. The children's father (Sethe's husband), Halle, has not been seen since 1885, the year of his failed attempt to escape from Sweet Home and ensuing descent into insanity. As Sethe explains to Paul D, who now suddenly shows up on the doorstep, Denver was born during the then-nineteen-year-old Sethe's own escape to Cincinnati at the same time. The ghost, she tells Paul D, is that of her elder daughter, whom she had sent "ahead with the boys" while still a nursing baby (11); before this we have learned that the baby's "rage" is due to its throat being cut, and that Sethe's having sex with the headstone engraver in exchange for his carving the word "Beloved" on her gravestone has done nothing to appease its "fury" (5–6). We are not yet told, however, that the baby's killer was Sethe herself.

Actions in the present – such as Sethe's washing chamomile sap from her legs or making biscuits – precipitate and are symbolically connected to memories of the past, such as the deceptive pastoral beauty of Sweet Home or the physical and sexual abuse to which its overseer, schoolteacher and his men had subjected the pregnant and lactating woman. Dialogue links the "here and now" – the flirtatious repartee of Sethe and Paul D or the sulky rejoinders of the lonely and envious Denver – with both the shared recollections of the reunited pair and an exchange of news that fills in their eighteen years apart. We are also privy to the individual consciousness of all three characters; their unspoken memories and thoughts interweave seamlessly with their spoken words and visible deeds. Color functions symbolically from the outset: Baby Suggs had spent her dying days pondering it, and the ghost makes her presence felt through a "pool of pulsing red light" (11). The very idea of a vengeful baby ghost connotes the Yoruban concept of the *abiku*, the wandering spirit of a dead young child, at the same time this ghost's palsying "fury" recalls the vengeance-bent Furies of the *Oresteia* (6). The audacious fusion of genres – gothic, psychological realism, classical epic, and tragedy – is established from the outset.

The rest of the novel's first part continues to interweave events in the novel's present with memories and exchanges of information about the past. Sethe refrains from telling Paul D exactly what she did until the last possible moment. As she begins a romantic involvement and sexual relationship with Paul D, as she deals with Denver's jealous impoliteness to him, and as the three, in a rare moment of familial bliss, enjoy a trip to a visiting carnival, she allows only for a future that consists of "keeping the past at bay" (51). She tells Paul D very little about the past: that soon after her escape the schoolteacher had "found" her, and that as she "wasn't going back there," she "went to jail instead" (50).

The effect on the reader of a mysterious female's sudden appearance – "a fully dressed woman walked out of the water" – anticipates the carnival goers' surprise in discovering this uncanny lady sitting outside their home (60). Water is highly symbolic at this moment: the newcomer who is about to declare her name as "Beloved" suffers from an apparently insatiable thirst, and Sethe urinates copiously (61). Denver is proprietorial about the guest from the outset, and both she and Sethe attempt to satisfy Beloved's appetite for stories about the family's past (69). Paul D is preoccupied by the woman's strangeness – she "acts sick ... but don't look sick" (67) – while Sethe and Denver both appear to sense who the visitor is, without daring to say so aloud. Moments when the three women enjoy a sense of rightful togetherness (for example, when rescuing rain-soaked laundry) are overshadowed by moments of unexpected violence and fear, for example, when fingers that Denver attributes to Beloved attempt to strangle Sethe in the Clearing. Beloved also gradually seduces Paul D: to his alarm and disgust, she persuades him to have sex with her repeatedly in the cold store, to "touch [her] on the inside part and call [her by her] name" (137).

The futility of Sethe's efforts to "beat back the past" is immediately apparent; every event or conversation opens the floodgates of memory. The near-choking in the Clearing, for example, causes Denver to recollect learning to read at Lady Jones's school, as well as a classmate's question that ended her attendance: "Didn't your mother get locked away for murder?" (123). While this question is significant as the first hint about Sethe's role in her baby's death, the continually unfolding picture of the events that both preceded and succeeded the cataclysmic attack emphasizes the inadequacy of such a description. Sethe's recollections stretch back to those of her own mother, whose name she never knew but who had survived the Middle Passage, who had loved Sethe but "threw away" the children fathered by the crew of the slave ship (74), who while a field laborer had taught Sethe to recognize her by the cross-and-circle branded under one breast, and who was killed in a group hanging. Roughly contemporaneous with Sethe's childhood must have been Baby Suggs's life as a slave: her household work for the Garners, her injury sustained during tobacco and rice work in Carolina before that, and the loss of all her children. With a sense of foreboding following her party to celebrate Sethe and Denver's safe arrival in Bluestone Road, Baby Suggs recalls her own earliest days of freedom, including the enthusiasm with which she began and the despair with which she abandoned the attempt to track down her offspring.

Sethe's intial sexual encounter with Paul D takes her back to her "wedding" with Halle and to the consummation of their love among the cornstalks. One of the most powerful recreations in the novel, meanwhile – the account of Denver's birth in a boat on the Ohio River – occurs in two separate sections. First, Denver recalls her abused and fleeing mother's rescue from her imminent death by a passing stranger, the vagrant white girl Amy Denver. Second, Denver tells Beloved about Amy's assistance at her birth. Sethe's desire to "lay it all down, sword and shield" (following Baby Suggs's advice, which itself echoes the song "I Ain't Gonna Study War No More") reminds her of her mother-in-law's inspirational preaching in the Clearing (102). While revisiting the Clearing herself, she remembers Stamp Paid's ferrying her across the Ohio River (a scene that revises Eliza's crossing the ice in *Uncle Tom's Cabin*) and her twenty-eight days of "unslaved life" (107; 111). Crucially, she recalls the development from "freeing" herself to "claiming ownership of that freed self" (112).

Paul D's memories are as broad as Sethe's are deep. Through his flashbacks and singing we learn of his surviving the abuses of the Georgia chain gang, his subsequent escape and wanderings, his fighting in the Civil War, and his encounters with vagrant black people "so stunned, or hungry, or tired or bereft it was a wonder they recalled or said anything" (78). Beloved herself, meanwhile, embodies the presence of the past, or the lack of clear distinction between "now" and "before." Whenever Denver asks her what it is like being dead, her replies consist of elliptical memories that suggest the Middle Passage ("hot," "dark," "the bridge") and that are more akin to ancestral memory – the experiences of her grandmother, Sethe's mother – than to her own lived experiences (88; 146).

As Sethe's relationship with Paul D deepens, she comes to believe that "her story was bearable because it was his as well – to tell, to refine, and tell again" (116). But the final three sections of part I – which give accounts of her attack from several contrasting perspectives – are testimony to the ways in which her actions evade reliable, objective narration. First, in an echo of the Book of Revelation's description of the Apocalypse, her behavior is perceived from the viewpoints of "the four horsemen ... schoolteacher, one nephew, one slave catcher, and a sheriff" (174). By foregrounding this narrative Morrison depicts (rather than describes) the brutal, racist culture from which Sethe wishes to save her children. The author delegitimizes the "master's voice" through tired but dangerous clichés: the slave catcher sees "a crazy old nigger standing in the woodpile with an ax" (175), and the schoolteacher and the nephew depart with relief from "the damnedest bunch of coons you ever saw" (177). Sethe's actual cutting of Beloved's throat gains dramatic intensity because it is not described here; it has already happened when the white folk arrive. When the proud, even hubristic Sethe (holding baby Denver) is driven away by the sheriff as the community hum, her exact deed has still not yet been "spoken." The revelation of the precise truth is again deferred by Paul D's denial that the newspaper account shown him by Stamp refers to Sethe. Morrison moves on to a strategy of revelatory "not-telling": she describes the details that Stamp does *not* share with Paul D about Sethe's hawklike murderous actions. In detailing that Paul D's disbelief causes Stamp to wonder whether it had really happened at all, that "a pretty little slavegirl ... split to the woodshed to kill her children" (186), Morrison finally articulates what Sethe did for the very first time.

Sethe's own explanation to Paul D circumnavigates the exact truth as she physically "spins" around her kitchen (188). She talks with apparent irrelevance of her isolation as a young mother, of the absence of those to whom she could turn for advice. But to emphasize both the universal nature of Sethe's motherhood and the specific violation of that state that slavery entails is of course exactly Morrison's point. Sethe interprets her violent actions as a logical extension of her self-determining escape from Sweet Home, as part of the way she claims herself and her right to real motherhood. The "hummingbird" sensation that she recalls at the moment of decisive action becomes a leitmotif in the rest of the novel (192). Her memory of her attempt to put her children "through the veil ... where no one could hurt them" – a moment of simultaneous rational and irrational action – recalls the narrative of the slave mother Harriet Jacobs (1865). Paul D, meanwhile, is "scared" by the wildness to which Sethe's "too thick" love has led (193). He leaves her, pretending he will return, but she is not deceived.

Part II

The second part's opening section privileges the consciousness of Stamp Paid, who notices that "124 was loud": with "hasty voices," with "mumbling," and with the word "mine" (199; 202–3). The trio of women inside, meanwhile – Sethe, Denver, Beloved – embark on the period of introverted, insatiable obsession with each other that is clearly doomed from the outset. The knell-like refrain that punctuates their skating trip, "nobody saw them falling" (205), imbues their mirth with hollowness and sets up the expectation of their imminent downfall.

Sethe's "click" of recognition about the true identity of Beloved, precipitated by the ghost-woman's humming of a privately shared lullaby (207), is reminiscent of the moment of *anagnorisis* ("recognition" /"discovery") that Aristotle defines as the turning point in Greek tragedy. Yet the happier that Sethe believes she has become, the more vulnerable and diminished she actually is. She feels she has found a "casket of jewels" (207); she senses "peace" (208); she locks herself and the girls in the snowed-under house, "wrapped in a timeless present" (234). Her subconscious is haunted by memories of her time with baby Denver in jail, however – of the difficulty of her escape from Sweet Home, of what she had witnessed of the schoolteacher's cruel violence and of his racist pedagogy. Morrison conveys Sethe's erroneous belief that Beloved's reappearance atones for past suffering, while the author implicitly questions whether any kind of atonement or recompense is possible at all.

Stamp Paid's memories, meanwhile, contribute to the "roaring" of a grossly abused and apparently unappeasable people (213). Beset by his recollections of Baby Suggs's defeated demise and death, and by the "stench" of white injustice and brutality that has plagued him all his life (212), Stamp appears to have reached a kind of impasse. Beloved and Denver refuse to open the door to his knocking, and Ella refuses to offer Paul D refuge in her home. The now-isolated and heavily drinking Paul D is consumed by destructive memories; the "tobacco tin" to which he confined his traumatic past has been "blown open" (258). He refuses both Stamp's apologetic offer of help and the older man's explanation that the infanticidal Sethe had only been trying to "outhurt the hurter" (276).

In an ironic play on the optimistic vision of Martin Luther King's "I Have a Dream" speech (1963), Morrison writes that the locked-in women of Bluestone Road were "free at last to be what they liked, … and say whatever was on their minds" (235). There follow interior monologues, extending over about twenty pages, that readers new to this author tend to find baffling and off-putting. Yet these four stream-of-consciousness sections – the first spoken by Sethe (236–41), the second by Denver (242–7), the third by Beloved (248–52), and the fourth by all three (253–6) – appear more intimidating than they are. Morrison is concerned here with the breakdown of meaning and coherence as much as she is with its creation, and for this very reason there are many lines for which a single fixed interpretation both cannot and should not exist.

Sethe's monologue lays claim to Beloved, conflating memories of the schoolteacher's abuse with expressions of grief about the baby's death and of joy in her present return. Addressed in part directly to Beloved and in part about her, it is an outpouring of exclusive love. In turn, Denver voices her fear of her mother, of the outside world, and of her bad dreams. She speaks of her longing for Baby Suggs and for her brothers, and of her conviction that her father will reappear. Beloved's monologue is the strangest: Morrison eschews punctuation, using only spaces to break up clauses. The ghost-woman's dislocated memories conflate recollections of her babyhood with those of being dead and with flashbacks to the gruesome conditions of the Middle Passage. These voice both the specific experience of Sethe's mother and the communal trauma of all enslaved Africans transported to the Americas. The unifying impulse is the desire for reconfiguration or reconstitution, for union or reunion: a fractured Beloved, returning gradually from an underwater death, longs both to be whole in herself and to "join" with her mother's "smiling face" (252). The final collaborative speech contains dialogues between each pair in the trio. The profound neediness with which the sterile, reiterated word "mine" is imbued resonates throughout Stamp's account of the sexual appropriation of his wife, Vashti, and Paul D's disbelieving contemplation of the apparently infinite nature of white brutality. The nadir is here, where part II draws to a close.

Part III

The novel's shortest and final part begins with the surprising news that "124 was quiet" (281), but 124 has also descended into chaos. Denver and her mother are starving, in a physical realization of their insatiable need to be loved and forgiven, while Beloved has grown fat by taking "the best of everything – first" (284). Sethe and Beloved now exclude Denver, while Beloved is also bent on Sethe's destruction. The ensuing crisis forces Denver to overcome her agoraphobia: she tentatively forges alliances first with Lady Jones, who ensures the community provides gifts of food, and then with the Bodwins, for whom she becomes a nighttime servant. This crucial reconnection with the outside world is the trigger to Denver's becoming an individual in her own right: Lady Jones's kindness "inaugurated her life in the world as a woman" (292), while Miss Bodwin encourages her to set her sights on Oberlin College (314). The self-assured young woman who holds her own with Paul D is a transformation of the lonely, jealous child we meet at the novel's opening.

Denver's actions ensure Sethe's salvation besides her own; they indirectly prompt Ella to lead the local women in their rescue mission. A narrative replete with Christian symbolism recounts a gothic but effective exorcism. The women gather "at three in the afternoon on a Friday," a time recalling the crucifixion of Christ (303). As they pray and, most importantly, sing, there is a sudden transition from past to present tense. Sethe rushes with the ice pick at the unsuspecting Mr. Bodwin because, in a flashback to the hummingbird-beak moment of the infanticide, she believes he has come to do harm either to her children or to her. At this moment the naked, hugely pregnant, vine-haired Beloved senses Sethe and Denver disappearing from her view, while in the eyes of the others, it is she who disappears from the porch. Morrison never clarifies whether her departure is of her own volition, or due to the community's actions, or to a combination of the two. Through this ambiguity the author leaves the novel's debate about the relationship between the individual and the community unresolved.

In yet another testament to the power of music, Paul D's return to Sethe and her recovery are signaled by his "chamomile" song. Paul D has learned that to pass judgment is a complicated and relative process, "like the time he worked both sides of the War" (315). Morrison pans one last time across the epic breadth of his travels in the Reconstruction years before zooming in on the most intimate of scenes: his persuading the broken, bedridden Sethe that she is her own "best thing," and that they should plan (a key word in this text) on "some kind of tomorrow" (322).

The epilogue to *Beloved* is one of the saddest and most beautiful passages in Morrison's oeuvre; it cries out to be read aloud. Here the focus has shifted away from Sethe, Paul D, and Denver, back to Beloved herself and her significance. In interviews and essays, Morrison often speaks with deep compassion of this baby who was murdered, and this epilogue, preoccupied with loneliness and forgetfulness, ensures that a mood of ambivalence persists at the novel's end. Beloved, "disremembered and unaccounted for" (323), stands for all those enslaved Africans and their descendants (the "Sixty Million and more" of the novel's dedication) whose lives and deaths are not remembered. Although they have "claim" – a desire for retribution, a right to atonement, or at the very least, recognition – they are not claimed. Their footprints, the traces they have left, are visible only to those who actively seek them by placing their own feet in the prints. The present tense in which four of the closing paragraphs are written creates the sense of perpetual loss, of the way the course of history has been permanently shaped by the fact of slavery and the countless lost lives it entailed.

A sentence that provokes fruitful debate is the refrain "It was not a story to pass on," which in its third repetition becomes "This is not a story to pass on" (322). Besides the paradoxical idea (occurring at the end of the sharing of this story) that this is not a story that should be shared, it may mean that the events or experience are not ones to repeat, or to relive. But opposite meanings are also there: this is a story that demands to be claimed – it is not one to pass over, nor one to "pass" racially on, to shirk by disowning one's racial identity.

The novel's final word, "Beloved," draws attention to the apparently infinite resonances of this character's name, and hence of her meaning. It recalls the words of God at the moment of Jesus's baptism: "This is my beloved Son" (Matthew 3:17), suggesting the redemptive power of Beloved, or of her return, and it brings the novel full circle by recalling the work's biblical epigraph from St. Paul's letter to the Romans (9:25). The echo of a Christian preacher addressing his or her congregation, "dearly beloved," suggests Morrison's addressing the congregation of her readers and testifies to her ambition to bear witness to, or to memorialize, transatlantic slavery as a whole. She explains the depth and breadth of this vocation in a 1988 interview, in words that have now become well known. "There is no place you and I can go," she says, "to think about or not think about, to summon the presence of, or recollect the absences of slaves. ... There is no suitable memorial or plaque or wreath. ... And because such a place doesn't exist, ... the book had to" (*DC* 44).

Jazz (1992)

This novel – the second in the trilogy, and a pitch-perfect performance – is predominantly set in 1920s New York. Its focus is the middle-aged couple, Joe and Violet Trace, who in 1906 migrate to the city from rural Virginia, where they had been agricultural laborers. The plot is relatively simple: in the fall of 1925, feeling isolated from the childless and depressed Violet, Joe embarks on a passionate love affair with the eighteen-year-old Dorcas, who is the niece of one of his beauty product customers. In January of the following year, apprised of her flirtations with men closer to her own age, Joe tracks down Dorcas at a party and shoots her. She dies from her injuries without revealing his identity. The narrator – a virtuoso character in her (or its) own right – opens the account with Violet's sabotage of Dorcas's face at her funeral, and the relationship between Violet and Joe appears irrevocably dysfunctional. Interwoven with descriptions of the violent recent past and the traumatic childhoods of both protagonists, however, is the story of their slow but steady progression toward reconciliation and a rebirth of mutual love and happiness.

While this novel's principal events can be relayed in just a few sentences, the dazzling sophistication of its execution, and its breadth and complexity as a voicing (or revoicing) of a specific moment or process in America's past, cannot. The rural dispossession and urban relocation of Joe and Violet recall those of the fictional Breedloves in *The Bluest Eye*, as well as the migration from the Deep South to Ohio of Morrison's own parents. Through her leading characters Morrison personalizes the period of transition and transformation that are historiographically labeled "the Great Migration" and "black urbanization." The author combines an unsentimental depiction of the abuses and failures that characterized the Reconstruction South with an equally frank representation of the realities of the poverty and discrimination that persisted in the free and urban North.

As Morrison outlines in her foreword, a photograph of a girl "shot by her sweetheart at a party," taken by the famed documenter of 1920s Harlem James Van Der Zee (and republished in the *Harlem Book of the Dead*), was her initial inspiration for the novel (*J* x). Yet her own portrayal of Harlem – which the narrator breathlessly terms "the City" – seeks out the tensions and contradictions within cultural narratives that attempt to mythologize and glamorize the era as "the Harlem Renaissance." Conventional literary history defines the Harlem Renaissance as a flowering of a new black aesthetic, corresponding with newfound economic independence and growth, and a movement encapsulated in Alain Locke's 1925 anthology *The New Negro*. In *Jazz*, Morrison complicates this through exploring the potential for both good and bad – in the ultimately inextricable realms of personal morality, political and economic conditions, and aesthetic expression – that urban freedom entailed. Her novel's title and its whole conception attest on one level, quite simply, to the music that (along with blues) both emerged from and defined this time of "radical change" (*J* x). On another level the title and the technique of the novel invoke jazz as a multifaceted metaphor for the intense and ambivalent nature of modernity itself. "I changed once too often," Joe Trace tells us ruefully, as he attempts to make sense of his actions. "You could say I've been a new Negro all my life" (129). In *Jazz*, Morrison shows that being black in a modernizing America both enabled and demanded endless reinvention and reexpression of the self. What did this actually mean for the individual players in that history?, she asks. What benefits did it bring, and what costs did it exact?

In the second of the ten unnamed sections that make up this novel, the narrator alternates between a close-up view of Joe and Violet, as they "train-dance" north on "the Southern Sky" (*J* 36, 30), and wide-angle shots of "a million others" who were similarly headed for the cities (32–3). The narrator might be speaking for herself, as well as for Morrison, when she observes that the new arrivals all "treated language like the same intricate, malleable toy designed for their play" (33). The prose of this text is replete with newly coined compound words – "citysky"; "going-to-bed-in-the-street clothes" (36; 55) – that indicate the ways in which new experience demanded a new language. Such innovative linguistic couplings also reflect the novel's organizing principle of hybridization or synthesis, of the making of new connections. The ubiquity of processes of dislocation and reformation is what makes this book so very much about modernism, in all its aesthetic forms, and about the role of African-Americans within that movement, as well as about the historical moment of modernity itself.

As do all her novels, *Jazz* conducts dynamic and revisionary dialogues with numerous other texts that have a stake in its subject. Morrison signifies on key works that have come to define the Harlem Renaissance: Claude McKay's *Home to Harlem* (1928), Jean Toomer's *Cane* (1923), Carl Van Vechten's offensively named *Nigger Heaven* (1926). The sections describing Golden Gray's origins and his search for his father and Joe's quest for his mother parody the genre of southern gothic and pastoralism. Perhaps most significantly, in a 2002 interview, Morrison states that "*Jazz* was [her] attempt to reclaim the era from F. Scott Fitzgerald" (*DC* 204). Critics have paid surprisingly little attention to the novel's dialectic with *The Great Gatsby* (published in the same year as Joe's shooting of Violet – 1926) or with the essay "Echoes of the Jazz Age" (1931), in which the male novelist uses jazz music to define an era and a generation while making only the most indirect of references to the African-Americans whose creation that music was. While Fitzgerald writes breezily of "bootleg Negro records" that "with their phallic euphemisms made everything suggestive,"[13] Morrison in turn relegates Fitzgerald's subjects, the "Long Island debutantes" whom jazz music "intoxicates ... more than champagne," to a passing reference two pages from her novel's end (*J* 227).

As I have already outlined, in Morrison's view jazz is at once sophisticated and accessible, as she intends her own writing to be. It is a democratic form involving multiple voices or instruments that converse with each other, that riff on a theme, in a kind of "call and response"; Morrison's narrative is modeled on this nonlinear, reiterative structure. As she outlines in her foreword, like her mother singing (and by implication like her own creative process), jazz "took from everywhere, knew everything," and "made it [its] own" (*J* xiii). In *Jazz*, the author, Morrison's narrator, and the people the narrator describes all remake their worlds in this way. As the author has stated, and as the following overview of the work's key presences – the City, the narrator, Violet, Joe, Golden Gray and Wild, Dorcas, and Felice – makes clear, "the project came as close as it could to its idea of itself – the essence of the so-called Jazz Age" (*J* xii). In other words, subject matter and form are inseparable. Morrison's reclamation of the Jazz Age embodies "the moment when an African-American art form defined, influenced, reflected a nation's culture" in myriad ways; the novel *is* the "improvisation, originality, change" that it describes (*J* xii).

The City

Morrison uses the term "the City" to refer specifically to Harlem, in a subversion of Fitzgerald's use of "the city" in *Gatsby*, where it means New York City as a whole. In the hands of Morrison's inventive, improvisatory narrator, "the City," even if not quite a character, is certainly a force to be reckoned with. "I'm crazy about this City," the narrator tells us (7), and her ensuing rhapsodies constitute energized descriptions of the urban environment: "Daylight slants like a razor cutting buildings in half. ... A city like this one make me dream tall. ... It's the bright steel rocking above the shade below that does it" (7). The novel repeatedly depicts striking human-and-architectural tableaux. It also juxtaposes euphoria about the novelty and energy of this urban, music-infused northern hub (it is "top-notch and indestructible," a place where "everything is ahead at last" (7)) with casually thrown-in details about the realities of continued discrimination and inequality (there are "no high schools" and "no banks" (8)). The description of the textures of Harlem life – "the beauty parlors, the barbershops, the juke joints, the ice wagons, the rag collectors, the pool halls" – testifies to Morrison's preparatory self-immersion in "every Colored newspaper [she] could for the year 1926" (*J* xi).

If spring, as the narrator tells us, is "when the City urges contradiction most" (118), then contradiction itself is what defines the City most. The novel at once engages and complicates the trope (exemplified by Frederick Douglass's paean to New Bedford in his 1845 *Narrative*) of the oppressed southern black's starry-eyed arrival in the utopian North. Morrison stages the newcomers' relationship with the city as a romance – they "fall in love" with it, and it is "forever" (*J* 33) – but this is a romance fraught with danger, as the lifestyle "pump[s] desire" rather than nourishing love (34). Early on, the narrator illuminates the City's paradoxical position as a place both of freedom and of unfreedom, and of both self-determined and predetermined fates: "The City makes people think they can do what they want and get away with it," she says (8). Yet on the same and immediately following page she emphasizes the City's controlling rather than liberating powers: you have to "pay attention to the street plans" (8), "to ... heed the design – the way it's all laid out for you" (9). Morrison's punning – evident in the key words "plans" and "design" – repays close scrutiny as the narrator waxes lyrical about "the range of what an artful City can do" (118). Faintly resonant of that Dickensian urban trickster "the Artful Dodger" (Morrison is an avid reader of Dickens), that the City is "artful" suggests at once its cunning and its aesthetic vitality. The City is full of art as well as artful: it *is* the story and the history it enables.

The Narrator

From her opening sentence, "Sth, I know that woman," this novel's narrator makes her commanding presence felt (3). Paradoxically, although she is self-analytical throughout the text and draws attention to the subjectivity of her individual perspective, we know nothing about the details of her life. Although we do not even know for certain that she is female, scholarly convention has always deemed her so, and there are several reasons for this. The first is that the speaker of the epigraph, "I am the name of the sound," which is from one of the Gnostic Gospel texts in the Nag Hammadi collection (discussed at more length in Chapter 3, "Morrison and African Cultures and Traditions"), is female.[14] The second is that Morrison might well choose a black female narrative voice as the most effective counterpoint to that of Nick Carraway, Fitzgerald's white male narrator of *The Great Gatsby*. The third reason has existed only since the foreword of 2005, for there Morrison takes pains not to distance herself but to ally herself with the narrator, declaring that "I know that woman" was her own frustrated exclamation as she struggled to begin the book (xiii).[15] In the novel itself, by hinting at and yet refusing to clarify her narrator's race and gender, the author posits a new and subversive "universal" or "norm."

Morrison has created the archetypal "unreliable narrator," one who even tells us while correcting her own account of Golden Gray, "I have been careless and stupid and it infuriates me to discover (again) how unreliable I am" (*J* 160). The speaker's self-reflexivity becomes the ultimate act of metafiction, a meditation on the power, responsibility, and fallibility of the creative mind and process. Aspiring to a transformative power, the narrator declares, "I have to alter things" (161) and confesses an authorial desire to make a better world: "I want to ... contemplate his pain and by doing so ease it, diminish it. I want to be the language that wishes him well" (161). Yet, in her self-confessed erroneous assumption that the Felice-Joe-Violet relationship would end in tragedy, she also questions the ethics of artistic representation, alluding to the literary predilection for gloom and doom that is sometimes an indulgent distortion of "reality." "Pain," she observes, "I seem to have an affection, a kind of sweettooth for it. ... What ... would I be without a few brilliant spots of blood to ponder?" (219).

In the same passage, the narrator comments on her taste for "bolts of lightning, little rivulets of thunder," continuing, "And I the eye of the storm" (*J* 219). These lines read at once as an ironic comment on her melodramatic inclinations, and as a sincere identification with the divine female speaker of "Thunder, Perfect Mind." Morrison's implied assertions about the sacred power and responsibility of the storyteller or writer here have much in common with the ideas she expresses in the Nobel Lecture written one year after the publication of *Jazz*. Despite an association with the divine, however, the narrator simultaneously impresses the reader as a lonely human observer, a character whose own romantic desires are unfulfilled. Early in the novel she recalls her partner's standing her up and falling asleep on her (9), and at its end she envies Joe and Violet their "public love" (229). It is here, just when the narrator's voice sounds most recognizably "real," her emotions most "human," that Morrison delivers her coup de grâce. We are asked to "look where [our] hands are. Now" (229); if we do so, we find they are holding the book. The narrator is suddenly illuminated as the book itself, as a reinvention of the "talking book" that, as Henry Louis Gates discusses in *The Signifying Monkey* (1988), is a key trope in African-American literary tradition. On one very important level, the romance, intimacy and creative partnership that the narrator craves and celebrates are those between the book and its reader.

Violet

When we first encounter Violet she is fifty years old, "awfully skinny," and possessed by vengeful rage about her husband's affair (*J* 4). Working intermittently as a casual hairdresser in her customers' homes, embarking on a short-lived retaliatory infidelity, she is preoccupied by the dead Dorcas, whose photograph sits hauntingly on the Traces' Lenox Avenue mantelpiece, and whom she futilely seeks to emulate. On the novel's second page, the narrator observes offhandedly that "the children of suicides are hard to please" (4). This is our first insight into Violet's childhood deprivations and losses. As the book progresses, through a combination of third-person narration and passages of contemplative first-person recollection, a clear picture of her traumatic early years in Virginia and the vagaries of her New York life emerges.

The themes of Violet's life are the classic Morrisonian themes: suffering, anger, resilience, and survival. From the narrator we learn of her recent "public craziness" and the "private cracks" in her sanity (*J* 22): releasing her pet birds (92), an alleged attempt to steal a baby, her insatiable "mother-hunger" resulting in her sleeping with dolls, and her later confusion as to whether Dorcas was "the woman who took the man, or the daughter who fled her womb" (108–9). From her visits to Alice Manfred we learn of her disappointed expectation about city life – she had thought it would be "bigger" (112). The novel's fourth section, in which she sits musing on her past and on her other, "Violent" self (*J* 75), reveals the happiness of her early years with Joe. Their early love had flowered despite the fact that when they met each other on a Virginian cotton plantation each was searching for another (his mother, in his case; the angelic Golden Gray of her grandmother's stories, in hers). It had survived her frequent miscarriages and their initial poverty on arrival in the city. The most striking passages in this section, however, concern Violet's memories of another solitary, brooding woman: her mother, Rose Dear, who had sat up waiting for the family's "dispossession" from the meager, post-Reconstruction homestead where she grew up (177). Violet recalls with shocking clarity the deprivation her large family faced, the brutality of the men who appropriated their every last possession, and the darkness of the well into which her mother had jumped. These scenes utterly destabilize any dominant cultural nostalgia about life in the "good old South"; there are no rose-tinted spectacles here.

Violet's suffering has made her a pitiable but by no means a pitiful figure. Morrison invests her dialogues – with Alice Manfred or with the contemptuous Cotown woman – with a tough and energizing brand of humor. The character's dynamic dialogues elevate rather than diminish her stature, and she articulates insights worthy of any tragic protagonist, for example, about her failure to maintain control of her own life. Violet is also redeemed by Felice's understated admiration for her: "Nothing she says is a lie" (*J* 205). In the novel's closing pages, the brief flashback to the Virginian shotgun house in 1906, in which Joe tenderly removes the work shoe of the exhausted and sleeping Violet, is a recollection striking for its uncustomary mood of peace and happiness. It is the perfect segue to the rich and contented "old-time love" that the Traces have achieved at the novel's end (228).

Joe

Joe's fellow cast members are quick to verbalize their assessments of his deeds. In her opening paragraph, the narrator tells us that his "deepdown, spooky love" for Dorcas "made him so sad and happy he shot her just to keep the feeling going" (*J* 3). We are also privy to the "trembling fury" and profound sense of betrayal felt by Alice Manfred about this apparently good man, respected and trusted in the community, turned "Murderer" after his affair with her niece (*J* 76). The novel as a whole, however, assembles a picture of Joe as a complicated, conflicted soul, one whom the reader struggles to judge harshly, and whose past apparently makes inevitable his volte-face in the significantly chosen "*fall* of 1925" (my emphasis), as well as its bloody denouement. Morrison's male protagonist operates as both a credible, psychologically realized individual and a mythical or archetypal figure.

The narrator's present-tense description of Joe's passionate, jazz-music-fueled relationship with Dorcas is erotically charged, conveying the act of intercourse through the rhythm of the dialogue: "Gimme this, I give you that," and so on

(*J* 39). At the same time, both the narrator's and Joe's own first-person accounts of the affair are replete with Edenic imagery. "You were the reason Adam ate the apple and its core," Joe declares of Dorcas (133). Morrison invokes the Creation story to emphasize the novelty, the newly found paradise that black urban life had the potential both to become and to lose and enlists the questions in Genesis about free will to explore the same in that modern world. A "faithful man near fifty," as the narrator declares, is at once "free to do something wild" (120) and "bound to the track" (120).

During his trysts with Dorcas, Joe tells her "things he never told his wife" (36), including his painful memories of his search for his mother, Wild. In his monologue about his seven new identities and through the narrator's reconstruction of his past, we learn of his being raised by the Williams family, naming himself "Trace" on learning that his parents had "disappeared without a trace" (124), and hunting during his boyhood with the woodsman hero Hunter's Hunter (also known as Henry LesTroy). Hunting is the motif that takes Joe's experiences to the realm of archetype: it links his loss of and search for his mother with his relationship with Dorcas and to his pursuit of her before he shoots her. (This connection is also manifest in the question and answer that link the novel's seventh and eighth sections, "Where is *she*? / There she is" (184–7)). The word "track," then, to which Joe is apparently bound, connotes at once the train track that enabled black migration, the jazz records that were symbiotic with that historical process, the tracks and tracking of the hunt, and even the idea of history (in the sense of "track record") itself. The word "trace" also bears some scrutiny, especially if you recall the penultimate paragraph of *Beloved*, where we are told that "by and by all trace" of the ghost is gone (*J* 324).

Joe's surname, with its Derridean resonances, implies that the writing of black history, the preservation (or destruction) of the past, is a complex act. Through Joe's three unsuccessful attempts to find and be recognized by his mother, Morrison expresses an ambivalence about African-American preoccupations with an idealized "home" or origin. Although Wild's "home in the rock" is a utopian space "both snug and wide open" that the narrator herself longs to possess (221), it is highly significant that on his second quest Joe "tripped over black roots" (179) and on his third he finds a tree "barren," with roots that climbed "backward, ... defiant and against logic" (182). The narrator suggests that Joe and Violet are most at home in their newfound present of the novel's end, where they talk signifying on both Douglass's *Narrative* and Zora Neale Hurston's *Their Eyes Were Watching God* (1937) – of "the Baltimore boats they never sailed on," and of the "pears they let hang on the limb" (*J* 228).

Golden Gray

"Back then, back there," Joe observes at the end of his monologue, "if you was or claimed to be colored, you had to be new and stay the same every day the sun rose and every night it dropped" (*J* 134). This expression of an apparently fruitless quest for a viable black identity picks up the defining predicament of the narrator in Ellison's *Invisible Man*, and it attests to the oppressive dominant culture of the post-Reconstruction South. In the "Golden Gray" sections of *Jazz* – the two parts that relate that young man's search for and confrontation with his father, Hunter's Hunter – Morrison refracts the world of postbellum southern gothic and melodrama through her subversive, parodic lens.

A brief iteration of this subplot may be useful at this point: Golden Gray is the pale-skinned son of Vera Louise, daughter of the (outwardly) upstanding white southerner Colonel Gray and of her black lover, whom we later discover to be Hunter's Hunter/LesTroy. The connection to Violet is that her grandmother, True Belle (whose name satirizes the concepts both of "true womanhood" and of the "southern belle"), was Vera Louise's maid, and hence the young boy's nanny; the connection to Joe is that Golden Gray encounters and rescues (against his finer instincts) the naked, pregnant, and injured Wild, just before she gives birth to Joe. The themes of this Golden Gray subplot are vintage "Old South": miscegenation, anxiety about paternity and racial identity, the conflict between propriety and desire. Southern "classics" such as D. W. Griffith's 1915 film *Birth of a Nation* and Faulkner's *Absalom, Absalom!* (1936) and *Light in August* (1932) are irreverently pastiched in these pages.

The choice of name, "LesTroy" (my emphasis), and the narrator's use of the present tense to describe Golden Gray's mission to find (and kill) his black father – "I see him in a two-seat phaeton" – mockingly engage the epic tradition that Griffith and Faulkner deploy sincerely (*J* 143). No literary genre or tradition is sacred in these passages: through Golden Gray's desire to "brag about this encounter, like a knight errant" (154), the author mocks the prevalence of the chivalric romance tradition in Confederate mythology. In the very next section, as well, Joe's quest for his mother draws on all the conventions of pastoral, before undermining that mode completely. The character recalls walking through an idyllic rural landscape, hearing "the music the world makes, familiar to woodsmen and shepherds" (176), but on his second search for his mother, when her singing breaks off, he is "disgusted" to smell "a mixture of honey and shit" (177). This counterpastoral continues in the depictions of the urban North, where Dorcas, who shares her name with a shepherdess in Shakespeare's pastoral romance *The Winter's Tale*, leads to anything but an idyllic, romantic life.

Dorcas and Alice

The backstories of Dorcas and of her aunt Alice give the central plot its breadth of historical, political, and sociocultural context. Dorcas was orphaned when her parents were killed in the East St. Louis race riots of 1917. The "heated control" of Alice's ensuing sanctimonious child rearing runs entirely counter to the liberalizing impulses of the 1920s and to the music in which those impulses were expressed (*J* 77). In Alice's view, Dorcas falls for Joe because he makes her feel older than she is (76), but the narrator also suggests they share a personal sense of emptiness, an "inside nothing," from the fact of the absence of their parents (38). Alice, meanwhile, experiences a range of different, impotent angers: at the racism to which the 1917 Fifth Avenue protest march draws attention, at the Traces' treatment of her niece, and, as we discover through one of her many intimate conversations with Violet, at her husband and his mistress. Alice's thoughts also form the entry to a memorable authorial meditation on the determined rage of women, nationwide, at this time: "Black women were armed; black women were dangerous and the less money they had the deadlier the weapon they chose" (77).

Through Felice, whose name (contradicting her own childhood struggles) means "happy," and who both is and is not a kind of Dorcas reincarnate, Morrison provides an unexpected critical perspective on the murdered girl.[16] Felice's insistence that Dorcas "let herself die" adheres to the idea of an individual's power to influence the outcome of his or her own life (209), and it ushers in the positive mood, the "something rogue," that characterize the novel's end (228). The narrator overturns her own belief that "the past was an abused record with no choice to repeat itself at the crack" (220), and the double meaning of "record" could not be more apposite. Ultimately, *Jazz* is a celebration of the human potential to be "original, complicated, changeable." Just like the eponymous music that these people in this time and place produced, they themselves are testimony to the processes "of invention, of improvisation, of change" (220; xiii).

Paradise (1998)

Morrison has often mentioned that her original title for *Paradise* was *War*. Set predominantly in rural Oklahoma, this last book in the trilogy does indeed stage many forms of conflict. There is a unifying thematic concern with physical violence on both an individual and a historical scale: depicting an America that is thoroughly bloodstained, the novel ranges from World War II to the shooting incident in 1976; from sexual and other acts of violence against women to the Vietnam War; and takes in the clashes between activists and law enforcement in the tumultuous 1960s along the way. Yet Morrison chose to call the novel *Paradise*.

The immediate counterpoint between this title and much of its subject matter reflects the nonphysical conflicts – the clash of ideas, ideologies, moral and historical viewpoints – that the story lines dramatize. In essence, the book is an exploration of how and why the purportedly upstanding male citizens of the small, all-black town of Ruby (which was founded in 1950 but boasts a proud prehistory) come to massacre a group of unarmed women. These women live in a so-called Convent (actually a former Indian school run by nuns) located seventeen miles away on the Oklahoma plain. The cast of the novel is huge: we meet a good many of Ruby's citizens besides its self-appointed leaders, the twins Steward and Deacon Morgan. We meet not only the lost or outlaw women who separately chance upon the Convent and decide to stay on there with its long-term resident, Consolata, but also the characters who determine the traumatic backstories from which these women have fled.

Ruby, by the 1970s, is a paradise manqué – it is a utopian project that, through its exclusivity and closed-mindedness, "carries the seeds of its own destruction" (*DC* 157). Morrison here configures a racially transposed allegory or inverted microcosm of the defining flaw of America's founding principles: the restriction of its opportunities and rewards to a carefully demarcated few. The fact that the massacre takes place in July 1976 (the bicentennial of the Declaration of Independence) and the names of citizens (such as *Jefferson* Fleetwood) testify to the ever-present interactions between the dominant culture of Ruby and that of the nation as a whole. This central storyline also speaks to the rise and fall of the flawed Thomas Sutpen in Faulkner's *Absalom, Absalom!*

There is an obvious opposition between the men of Ruby, who are patriarchal, defensive of their racial "purity," religiously and morally conservative, inward-looking, and inhospitable, and the women at the Convent, who are self-sufficient without men, whose racial identities are named neither by themselves nor by Morrison, who are liberal in their moral and religious views and practice, and who are welcoming and solicitous to outsiders. Yet the Convent is no paradise either: towards the novel's end, these women come close to self-annihilation. To conceive of this novel as a series of juxtapositions or polarities that we must categorize as either "right" or "wrong" is therefore to misread it. Morrison exposes the dangers of rigid binary thinking, or of action based on polarized principles. She is more interested in the interactions between the Convent and Ruby than in their dissimilarity, in the (lost) potential for a mutually beneficial symbiosis than in the defeat of either one by the other.

Critics have paid relatively little attention to a third narrative strand or sphere in this story – the one that disrupts the Ruby/Convent dichotomy and that makes an "either/or" interpretation of the work an impossibility. This crucial third element is the lives and the worlds of the four deracinated women – Mavis, Gigi (or Grace), Seneca, and Pallas – *before* they each arrive at the Convent, and the transformed version of these worlds to which they return, themselves transformed or resurrected, at the novel's end. The account of Mavis's loss of her infant twins and her abusive, psychosis-inducing marriage, or of Seneca's attempts to survive as an abandoned child, reveal Morrison's often-overlooked power as a chronicler of domestic unhappiness. The experiences of these women before they arrive at their Oklahoman sanctuary sets the Ruby-and-Convent drama in broader context: their lives embody, in different ways, both the failure of the "American dreams" of freedom, wealth, progress, and happiness, and the pertinacity of those dreams. Each woman subverts the paradigm of the traveling male hero (epitomized by Sal Paradise in Kerouac's *On the Road* (1955)) by ending her self-proclaimed mission to California or Mexico (or elsewhere) in the middle of an Oklahoman "nowhere."

The Past

Paradise is a novel about the dangers inherent in mythology and mythmaking; like all Morrison's works, it is about the invested and contested nature of the making of history itself. The author constructs an implicit dialogue between Ruby's founding myth and the historical and mythological narratives of quest and utopian settlement that enjoy hallowed status in American culture: Moses leading the Israelites to the Promised Land, the Pilgrim Fathers at Plymouth Plantation, the Puritans of Massachusetts Bay, the Mormons in Utah, and so on. While she attributes to Ruby "the characteristics, the features of the Old Testament" (*DC* 157), she constructs *Paradise* as a kind of countertestament. The nine chapters, in which the narrative voice is predominantly third-person and omniscient, are named for nine women characters: "Ruby," "Mavis," "Grace," "Seneca" et al. This revisionary echo of the male-named biblical books such as "Job" or "Isaiah" emphasizes the relationship between women and the divine that is a central concern in this text.

We learn most about the history of Ruby's founding families from the novel's fourth section, named "Seneca." Here the narrative privileges the thoughts of first Dovey Morgan; then of her husband, Steward; of Dovey's sister, Soane (married to Deacon); and finally of Deacon, in the course of one evening and the following morning in October 1973. Driving into town to open his bank, Deacon thinks back to Haven, the town the previous generation had abandoned in 1949, before the foundation of Ruby one year later. Thinking of his childhood home, he recalls "listening to war stories; to stories of great migrations – those who made it and those who did not; to the failures and triumphs of intelligent men. ... All there in the one book they owned then" (*P* 110–11) We do not realise Deacon is recalling the Bible until he describes the physical nature of the treasured book; the stories of war, migrations, heroic exploits, and love could belong to any mythology or national cultural memory. While Morrison's frequent observations about the central place of the Bible in her own childhood resonate here, through the Rubyites' preoccupation with and reiteration of their own heroic heritage, the author explores the impulse to turn personal experience into quasi-classical or biblical epic. The citizens' investment in their creation myth and their penchant for memorialization of the past epitomize a quintessential Morrisonian dilemma: how can we, as human beings, and/or as Americans, and/or as black Americans, exploit the necessary and beneficial aspects of the stories of our lives without being imprisoned or calcified by them?

Paradise reveals the details of the past incrementally during the novel's progressing present. Once again the reader must assemble the pieces, yet this book is distinctive for the fact that its characters tell the same details, sometimes even in the same words, over and over again. As readers we may find the memories of the Morgans somewhat sermonic and ponderous at times, because Morrison positions her readers alongside the jaded young Rubyites who are suffocated by the Elders' unchanging and "controlling" accounts of the past (*P* 13). In the opening chapter, "Ruby," we learn of the "Old Fathers" who trekked "from Mississippi and ... two Louisiana parishes to Oklahoma" in the 1880s–90s (14; 13) and who label their 1890 exclusion from Fairly, Oklahoma, "the Disallowing" (13; 95;109). As Sharon Jessee has shown, Morrison's narrative is clearly grounded in the historical record of thirty-plus all-black towns (such as Nicodemus, Langston, or Boley) founded in Kansas and Oklahoma in the decades the novelist describes. The unwelcoming newspaper slogan of ancestral memory, for example, "Come prepared or not at all" (14), is a verbatim use of the caption heading an actual notice that "ran continually in *The Langston Herald*" in 1894–5.[17]

The story has all the elements of religious or folkoric myth: heroes who demonstrate resilience, the making of huge sacrifices in the overcoming of adversity, the visionary appearance of "the leader" (anticipating the spiritual figures who make visitations to both Dovey and Consolata) who indicates to Big Papa where Haven should be built (*P* 98). Haven rises and falls like a tragic hero in its own right, but through the overblown, almost caricatured names of key players and moments in the dynasty – "Big Daddy" (95), "Big Papa" (95), the "Grand Tour" of 1910 (102) – Morrison gently mocks the overdetermined and overinvested nature of Ruby's origins narrative. The eclectic combination of classical, biblical, and Puritan names boasted by its citizens – from Cato to Juvenal and Apollo; from Zechariah and Peter to Charity and Shepherd – contributes to the sense of a community in which psychologically realized individuals risk becoming archetypes trapped within myth and legend.

Haven becomes nothing less than an ideology: "the idea of it and its reach" inspires its second-generation citizens to survive their active service in World War II and to go on to found Ruby in 1950. Ever since then, Deacon and Steward have conceived of their new town, named for their sister, who died on the journey there, as "the one black town worth all the pain" (5). Steward's unshakable conviction that the dissenting views of the younger generation need be neither listened to nor accommodated is rooted in his belief that the youngsters have "no notion of what it took to build this town" (93).

The Present

Presiding in silent fury over Arnette and KD's wedding in 1974, the Baptist minister Richard Misner – whose "sensibility about moral problems" Morrison once identified as "closest to her own" (*DC* 141) – muses on the causes of "the town's unraveling" (161). He regrets the townsfolk's preoccupation with their ancestors, "as if past heroism was enough to live by" (161). Certainly the novel's "present," from 1968 to 1976, does not depict Ruby or its Elders in a favorable light, nor the community as flourishing. Dovey notices of her husband that "the more [he] acquired, the more visible his losses" (82), and among these losses are their infertility, the deaths of their nephews (Deacon and Soane's sons) Easter and Scout in Vietnam, and the imminent cessation of the family name. Ironically, the ruling generation's preoccupation with purity of blood, with the blackness of "8-rock" skin, and with intermarriage between the founding families, which are all inverted imitations of white racist practice, have led to a pervasive sterility. In the course of her ultimately abortive family tree project, Pat Best uncovers dark secrets about incestuous marriages between the founding families. The sickness of the Fleetwood babies dramatizes the logical end point of isolated, inward-looking exclusivity.

The ruthless self-centeredness of the Morgan twins, evidenced by their unwillingness to give financial support to their less-prospering fellow citizens, contributes to an ethos that generates the town's catastrophes. Steward and Deacon also exacerbate the rebelliousness of the younger generation by reacting to their dissent with the threat of violence. During the meeting at the Calvary Church in October 1973, the young people insist that the motto on the Oven (that sacred and monumental symbol of Ruby's civic pride) ought to read, "Be the Furrow of His Brow." This expresses their sense of themselves as God's "instrument, His justice," in the civil rights struggles of the decade (87). The Elders' insistence on "Beware" expresses their adherence to a disciplinarian, vengeance-seeking Old Testament–style God, and they demonstrate these characteristics themselves in their inability to tolerate ambiguity or controversy. Steward's last word on the matter to the young people says it all: "If you … ignore, change, take away, or add to the words in the mouth of that Oven, I will blow your head off just like you was a hood-eye snake" (*P* 87).

The Oven – former focal point for community and religious rituals, now somewhat redundant as a "utility" turned "shrine" (103) – becomes the site of the young people's struggles for both their political and moral self-determination. The youths take to drinking there, and they dance there provocatively with the Convent girls at the wedding party, but one of their number also paints on it the raised fist of the Black Power movement (101). Through fleeting references to Anna Flood's, Richard Misner's, or Gigi's history of activism and through the fact that Mavis arrives at the Convent in the month of Martin Luther King's assassination (April 1968), Morrison creates a sense of historical and political realities pressing in on the isolated worlds of Ruby, "deafened by the roar of its own history" (306), and of the Convent. While the reactionary New Fathers strive to keep out the radical politics and instability sweeping the nation as a whole in these years, Misner and his young followers try to maintain a stake in the "black is beautiful" movement and in the identification with an originary African homeland, and to engage with "Du Bois problems" rather than the "Booker T solutions" favored by the town's Elders (212). To emphasize this friction, Morrison interweaves Pat's and Richards's discussion of politics and change with the performance of the ideologically burdened Christmas play, in which the "Holy Family" has been replaced by the founding "holy families" of Ruby (215).

For the younger generation of women, life in Ruby appears scarcely viable. Billie Delia flees to an independent life in Demby, while Arnette, whose prematurely forced first baby died at the Convent in 1970, commits to a future with K. D. only through a series of self-deceptions and compromises. Through the lives of the older female generation, now in their forties –Soane, Dovey, Mable Fleetwood – Morrison explores the complexities of freedom, of power, and of their absence. The author notes that the men's newfound financial security, combined with the technological advances of the 1950s and early 1960s, enables the women to enjoy the apparent liberations (such as the luxury of time) that household appliances give them. In the comically sexualized under-tones with which the author describes the new kitchen gadgets, however – "humming, throbbing ... softly purring" (89) – she questions whether their liberation is genuine. The patronizing male view that women are "always the key" (a pseudocomplimentary but unconsciously apposite observation) leads to their oppression not their freedom (61): their husbands ultimately prize them only for their reproductive powers and hence guard jealously their chastity and purity.

Along with a few exceptional men, the women unambiguously hold the moral high ground in this town. It is only they who donate money to Richard Misner's civil rights causes, and it is they, led by the aptly named Lone Du Pres, who seek to stop the massacre. During her nighttime drive back from the Convent, after warning its residents about the men's plotting, Lone realizes that "it was women who walked this road. Only women" (270). While the men drive out there to satisfy their own desire for spices or sex, the act of walking the road, and the interactions between Ruby and the Convent that the women generate, are central to the salvation of many. The New Fathers tell themselves that "everybody who goes near [the Convent] is maimed somehow" (276), but it is in fact the already-maimed – Soane, Arnette, Sweetie, Billie Delia, as well as its five longer-term inhabitants – who find sanctuary, meaningful friend-ships, and restorative healing within its walls. By juxtaposing the genuinely safe and tolerant space of the Convent, with its welcoming kitchen and plenti-ful food, against the apparently ordered but dangerously repressed space that is Ruby, with its no-longer-functioning Oven, Morrison illuminates the elusive and paradoxical nature of "home."

In the chapter that bears her name, Consolata's view of the women in her care prevents naive interpretations of the Convent as a realized utopia. The older woman, in her own wine-soaked despair, reflects on the "disorder, deception" and "drift" that unify the "broken girls" who use her as a confessor, divulging to her their "babygirl dreams" (222). Her recollection of her own life story – she was an orphan rescued from the abusive streets of a South American city and taken to the "Christ the King School for Native Girls" (224) – explains the culturally hybridized means by which she brings about the recuperation of her charges. At the prompting of Lone Du Pres, Consolata discovers she is gifted with "in sight" (247), special powers whereby through "stepping in" she can restore the dead to life (245). In spite of her passionate affair with Deacon and its ending, she first "practices" this power in resurrecting his son, Scout, who has died in a car crash (245). Her unorthodox theology promotes a reconnec-tion between the physical and the spiritual, between the earthly and the divine, that overturns the polarization between the two in conventional Christianity and that has much in common with both traditional West African beliefs and their retention in New World Voudoun.[18]

Also resonant in Consolata's outlook is the divine female speaker in the Nag Hammadi text, "Thunder, Perfect Mind," from which (as she does in *Jazz*) Morrison takes the epigraph to this novel. The significance of these lines, "for many are the pleasant forms," is at least threefold in the novel. First, their sentiments echo Consolata's insistence on salvation through the body rather than in escape from it – a premise that the ritual drawing of and on the body templates enacts. Second, they join their own syncretic nature to the rituals derived from Candomblé (African-Brazilian tradition) such as the women's cathartic dancing, thereby fusing one already-hybridized tradition or outlook with another. Third, they contribute to the novel's investment in the powerful identification between womanhood and divinity that runs counter to the patriarchy of the Methodist and Pentecostal churches in Ruby and of the imperialist version of Roman Catholicism that informed the practices of the erstwhile girls' school.

The Future

The visiting stranger who precipitates Connie's conducting of the healing rituals – the cooking, the "loud dreaming" (264), the template drawing, and the dancing – has affinities both with the newly resurrected Christ and with the Candomblé god Eshu Elegbara.[19] Together with Consolata's vision of a paradise that is strongly suggestive of Brazil, this transnational spirituality could hardly be more different from Ruby's predominant religious culture. Yet it is important not to overlook the radical and unorthodox religious presences that play a key role even within that town. To attend to the words and thoughts of Richard Misner, too, is to encounter a radical liberation theology, an emancipatory interpretation of the Christian Gospel. The crucified Christ, in Misner's view, is one of many "death row felons" whose "official murder ... moved the relationship between God and man from CEO to supplicant to one on one" (*P* 146). To this minister, the cross is not a sign of racial or ethnic exclusivity but one that diverse cultures have in common: "all had a finger memory of this original mark" (145). The broadmindedness of Misner; of his wife-to-be, Anna Flood; of Lone; and in their own ways of Dovey and Soane is surely what makes the town's postmassacre salvation a possibility.

When the New Fathers open fire at the Convent, with "God at their side .... For Ruby," they entertain no doubts and tolerate no ambiguities (*P* 18). During the nighttime choric discussions that Lone overhears at the Oven, the men "mapped defense" of their hometown, and "honed evidence" for its need (275). Employing the imagery of miasma, or pollution, they associate the women

with every possible contaminant, and in an act of scapegoating that far sur-
passes the community's treatment of Sula in *Sula*, they blame the Convent
women for each and every one of the "intolerable ways" in which Ruby was
changing (275). Here Morrison adds psychological exploration to what she
has called the "seed" of the book: a real historical occurrence she had heard
about in Brazil, in which "some black nuns occupying a Convent near a small
town were shot by local residents for practicing what the attackers claimed
were pagan rites."[20]

One of Morrison's central themes here is hypocrisy. First, she exposes the
hypocrisy of morally imperfect protagonists such as Deacon Morgan, who is
desperate "to erase both the shame" of his affair "and the kind of woman he
believed was its source" (279). Second, in the novel's opening section, which
functions on one level as an allegorical critique of the heavy-handed workings
of the American state, the author reveals the voyeurism and irrational violence
(akin to that of Pentheus in Euripides's *Bacchae*) of those who claim to act in
the name of law, order, and decency. As they scour the Convent building with
their torches, titillated by the remnants of the erotic foibles left by the mansion's first owner, Morrison depicts them as hungry for the "filth" they wish to
eradicate (3). The much-discussed opening sentence, "They shoot the white
girl first" (3), expresses both the gunmen's clarity of purpose and the ambiguity to which their actions lead. By never revealing which convent dweller the
"white girl" is, Morrison simultaneously criticizes the New Fathers' obsession
with race and strips any racially demarcated worldview such as theirs of its
power.

The ensuing absence of the dead bodies, together with the indifference of
law enforcement, allows for competing narratives about what happened and
enables the "second chance" that God appears to have given the town (*P* 297).
The "outrageously beautiful, flawed and proud people" now operate both as
suddenly insightful fallen tragic heroes and as repentant sinners (306); Deacon
Morgan, who walks barefoot to confide in Misner, is at the forefront of this
moral rebirth and is at last distinguished from his less penitential but more
sinful brother, who actually fired the shot into Consolata's skull. The need to
bury the body of the infant Save Marie indicates the town's new grounding
in the realities of human existence rather than the perpetuation of an unat-
tainable mythical ideal. Until now, in a powerful counterpoint to the opening chapter of *The Scarlet Letter*, Ruby had prided itself on needing neither a
prison nor a cemetery.

Morrison gives the final chapter of her book not to Ruby but to the women
who have transcended its treatment of them through their mysterious resur-
rection. Our final perspective on the town is via Billie Delia, who imagines

the murdered women returning with "blazing eye" and "warpaint" to avenge themselves on their killers, in the manner of Aeschylan Furies (308). But the final pages of *Paradise* discredit such urges for reciprocal violence, in that the women have no interest in revenge. Billie's fantasy is dispelled by the description of each resurrected woman absolutely at peace, getting on with her new, healed life, and giving Ruby and its citizens never a backward glance.

The novel's final page is a coda, a present-tense tableau of Consolata with the spiritual mother from her homeland, Piedade, who now sings a song of "solace" (318). *Piedade* is Portuguese for "piety" or "compassion," and the image of her cradling Consolata constitutes a revised version of the pietà, the conventional depiction of the Christian madonna and child.[21] While Misner's Christ is black, Morrison's here is female, and while there is critical resistance, in some quarters, to identifying in Morrison's work an endorsement of the key tenets of the Christian Gospel – repentance, forgiveness, redemption – the ending of *Paradise* illustrates that to ignore this impulse in her work is to distort it. Ultimately, this novel suggests that a Christianity open to syncretism, and one stripped of the dominant ideologies of racism, imperialism, and patriarchy that have pragmatically harnessed it, is a faith fraught with radical potential.

Love (2003)

Love is as much about power as it is about love. Its primary setting is the fictional town of Silk and its environs, which are located on the southeastern U.S. coast. The action of the novel's present occurs in the 1990s, making this book the most contemporary in its setting of the oeuvre to date. *Love* is, on the one hand, about how its elderly women protagonists, Heed and Christine, were shaped by and perceive the past, and, on the other, about the apparent indifference of Romen, the fourteen-year-old male protagonist, and of his sixteen-year-old girlfriend, Junior, to the nature of the world before they were in it. Principal themes are the changing nature of the United States during the unfolding twentieth century and the complex status of African-Americans (in particular black women) during the transition from segregation to integration.

The novel's opening voice is that of L, a female narrator whose italicized prose comes to us from beyond the grave, in that she died in 1976. L stands for "Love" itself – "*the subject of First Corinthians, chapter 13*" (*L* 199; original italics) – and her account of her watery birth identifies her strongly with Venus/Aphrodite of Graeco-Roman tradition. From its opening sentence her prologue suggests the simultaneous power and vulnerability inherent in women's sexuality, but the nine succeeding chapters for which it sets the scene are all named for one man: Bill Cosey. This deceased but legendary local hero, founding owner of the now-dissipated but once glamorous Cosey's Hotel and Resort (6), is construed variously as "Friend," "Stranger," "Benefactor," "Lover," "Husband," "Guardian," "Father," and "Phantom" by those who knew him. The entire community participates in the construction of his mythical identity: his wives (first Julia, then Heed); his lovers (the "sporting woman" Celestial and numerous others (188)); his son, Billy Boy, who died before his father, in 1935; Billy Boy's once-competent, then insane, and now dead wife, May; Cosey's granddaughter, Christine; and his erstwhile employees, who include L (former chef at the hotel) and Romen's grandparents, Vida and Sandler Gibbons. The newcomer, Junior, meanwhile, performs her life for her imaginary version of Cosey, for the "Good Man" that he is in her fantasies (156).

Junior first encounters Cosey through his portrait, and it is in this first chapter, "Portrait," that we begin constructing a narrative about the past from the piecemeal clues we are given in the present. From L's prologue we have learned of the changes time has brought to the neighborhood (the collapse of the resort, the development of the more impoverished Up Beach area) and of the embattled and battling "Cosey women" who live in the Monarch Street mansion (*L* 9). As June meets both her new employer, Heed, and the vengeance-bent Christine; or as Romen chats about the past over dinner with his grandparents, the multiple and conflicting accounts of Cosey begin to accumulate. As the novel unfolds, the reader struggles to make sense of the "county's role model" (37) and of the effects that he had on those who lived in his shadow. Was he the "wonderful man" that Heed claims (26)? Or is Christine's memory the one we should trust? She recollects him as "the Big Man who, with no one to stop him, could get away with … anything … he wanted" (133).

There may be some truth in Vida's story of heroic downfall – that Cosey was "a commanding, beautiful man surrendering to feuding women, letting them ruin all he had built" (36). Yet Morrison encourages us to read between these lines, presenting us with an uncompromising critique of patriarchy and its effects in both domestic and political spheres. In L's mind, Cosey's fate is a story of feminist triumph – of "*how brazen women can take a good man down*" (10; original italics). Yet at the novel's end a sense of unfulfilled longing and irrevocable loss persists. As the two decrepit but reunited friends, Christine and Heed, realize with quiet but profound pain, "[they] could have been living [their] lives hand in hand instead of looking for Big Daddy everywhere" (189). Through their strange story, the novelist weighs the costs against the rewards of the different choices that we make, or that are made for us, in love's name.

One of the first questions that Heed asks June, when interviewing her for the post of "companion, secretary," is "Can you keep a secret?" (27). The novel's plot accumulates in a series of long-held secrets now disclosed to the reader. We learn, for example, that Christine and Heed's precious girlhood friendship was destroyed not just because Cosey made the outrageous decision that Heed, an eleven-year-old member of the disreputable Johnson family, would be his second wife (making her suddenly Christine's step-grandmother), but also because both girls had already been subjected to his transgressive sexual behavior at an even younger age. Near the novel's end we discover that Cosey had once molested the nine-year-old Heed and that Christine had observed his ensuing masturbation in her own bedroom; until now the women had "never been able to share [this] certain twin shame" (190). After the cataclysmic wedding, Christine had been sent to boarding school and felt usurped from her own home; Heed, meanwhile, felt permanently inadequate because of her near-illiteracy and humble origins. She struggled to survive the wiles of vengeance-seeking May and the financial demands placed on her by the business's collapse following Cosey's death.

In "Portrait" the two women, now in their sixties, are barely able to coexist under the same roof. They have been feuding, we discover, since their graveside fight at Cosey's funeral. While Romen helps them with manual tasks, the arrival of "homeless, rudderless" June (198) leads to heightened tension in the house. This is not just because she and Romen embark on a passionate sexual affair, but because her role is to assist Heed in finding – or fabricating – legal proof that it is the widow and not the granddaughter who is the rightful and intended inheritor of Cosey's wealth. Through reconstructions of the past that in turn privilege the viewpoints of L, of May, and of Vida and Sandler, besides those of Christine and Heed, Morrison explains how the two old women come to confront each other in the attic of the old hotel. Their conflicting claims to Cosey's legacy become quite literally a fight to the death, in that Heed falls through the attic floor and enjoys only a brief reconciliation with her former friend before she dies from her injuries.

The obvious symbolism of Heed's fall exemplifies the highly allegorical and symbolic character of the novel as a whole. The author examines the nature of gender conflict, of class struggle, of intra- as well as interracial discrimination, of insanity and physical violence, of loyalty, and betrayal, love, and hatred as they materialize within and affect one family, community, and town, but also in the world at large. The novel operates as a fable about the nature of America itself – about its discovery and colonization, and about its recent imperialist role on the global stage. Through the fact that Cosey embodies the fulfilment of the American Dream, in all its flaws as well as its glamour, Morrison calls into question both the nature of the nation's self-defining ideology and the way that ideology is formed. Thus while this text is on one level about sexual violence against women – it is structured around acts of rape and unified by anxiety about rape – on a second level rape functions symbolically. The novel implies both that the European colonization of America was a kind of rape, and that the United States of the late twentieth century acted in the manner of an unchecked sexual predator that, like Cosey, could "get away with … anything [it] wanted" (*L* 133).

In a 2003 radio interview, Morrison says that her "seed" for *Love* was the image of Pretty-Fay and her "little white-mitten hands" as she was being raped by Romen's friends: she goes on to explain that her aim in writing about the act of rape is to "sabotage" the "male pride … in the language" that characterizes rape scenes "from the rape of Lucretia" onward.[22] The author's depiction of Junior (molested by the administrator of the Correctional) and Christine (whose activist boyfriend turns a blind eye to a colleague's raping a volunteer), as well as of Pretty-Fay, suggests the ubiquity of male sexual aggression. It also eschews reinscription of these violations by renouncing an intrusive authorial gaze and other conventional narrative methods. In the gang rape scene, for example, Morrison diminishes "male pride" by depersonalizing the rapists, reducing them to a series of nameless "naked male behinds" (49), and forces us to encounter the victim's vantage point, "face . . turned to the wall and hidden beneath hair undone by writhing" (46).

Cosey's behavior toward Heed is harder to judge and is one of the many morally ambiguous elements in this text. Is he a bullying pedophile who buys himself a child with whom to fulfill his lurid fantasies, or is he (as Heed herself believes) a benevolent, considerate protector who rescues her from the vulnerability of poverty and the advances of others? Sandler finds Cosey's sexual promiscuity disturbing, yet is there a redemptive quality to his passion for Celestial, given that Celestial herself embodies a redemptive force? L confesses (to the reader only) to having poisoned Cosey and to having forged the notes that fuel the feud between Christine and Heed; did she, in fact, rescue the women from a tyrant, or did she precipitate their downfall? Morrison – in her exploration of the relationship between excessive reason and excessive passion, between unenforceable prohibitions and total moral relativism, between the discretion and sexual restraint that the elderly L favors and the indiscretion and extravagant indulgence that Romen and Junior favor – portrays the confusions and errors inherent in the transition from old ways to new. L looks back almost fondly to the archaic old law embodied in the monstrous, vengeful spirits known as "Policeheads" of local folklore, and it is true that the modern system for maintaining order (referenced by Cosey's destroyed will, or the lawyer whom Christine visits in vain) appears no more successful.

The author suggests that the women have one thing in common despite the changes all around them: each must struggle to survive in a world "organized around the pressing needs of men" (*L* 92). The costs of this struggle are not small. May pays with her sanity, and Christine and Heed lose their innocent friendship in competing for Cosey's favor. Christine's harsh words in their secret language, Idagay (which translate as "You a slave! He bought you with a year's rent and a candy bar!" (129)), testify to the violation of the erstwhile bond between them. At the same time, and without diminishing the intensity of her challenge to the ubiquitous patriarchal culture, Morrison sympathetically depicts Romen's fraught search for a viable masculine identity. Convinced that the brutality of his peers signifies a heroism that he himself lacks (because he releases Pretty-Fay), it is not until the novel's end, after his attempted rescue of Heed and Christine, that he realizes his own worth.

Morrison's evaluation of the civil rights movement in this novel is complex and nuanced. She explores two different problems that it entailed: the losses or decline in quality of life that integration, paradoxically enough, brought to black communities; and the patriarchy or misogyny inherent in the process of the struggle itself, in which women's rights were subordinated and compromised in the cause of racial advancement. As she writes in the foreword, "Beneath ... the surface story of ... the struggle for integration ... lies another one: the story of disintegration – of a radical change in conventional relationships and class allegiances that signals both liberation and estrangement" (*L* xi). While the author is keenly attuned to the dangers of nostalgia, her depiction of Cosey's Resort as one that flourished during the depression and during segregation and that collapsed after integration forces us to avoid glib, unqualified endorsement of the post-1960s world. While L suggests it was Cosey's transgressive second marriage, rather than "civil rights, integration," that precipitated the demise of his business (105), through the class prejudices and snobberies that underlie the interactions among Christine, Heed, Junior, and the lawyer, Gwendolyn, Morrison explores the end of "pre civil-rights intimacy" and of black cultural cohesion (*L* xi).

The author examines the difficulty individual women faced in negotiating a path through the political minefield that was the 1960s. May, for example, is bewildered and disoriented to discover that her prosegregation stance becomes "no longer old-time racial uplift, but separatist, 'nationalistic.' Not sweet Booker T., but radical Malcolm X" (80). The general sense of confusion is brilliantly conveyed in Heed and Christine's final conversation as they await rescue in the hotel: "We sold ourselves to the highest bidder," Christine says.

"Who you mean 'we'"?, asks Heed, "Black people? Women?" "I don't know what I mean," is the response (185). Christine's self-annihilating involvement with the movement exposes the ways in which negotiations of racial progress demanded the oppression of women. Her relationship with Fruit follows an old-time patriarchal model, and Morrison's depiction of her entrapment within "civil disobedience and personal obedience" (167) reflects the sexism within civil rights activist groups that is documented by Angela Davis in her autobiography (which was edited and published by Morrison in 1974), and by Michele Wallace in *Black Macho* (1978).

When May writes to Christine that "CORE is sitting-in in Chicago," Christine asks herself, "Who was she, this Cora?" (97). The punning on pronouncing the acronym for the Congress of Racial Equality as "Cora" brings to mind the Greek myth of Kore (or Persephone, in Roman tradition), often anglicized to Kora, with which Morrison engages in *The Bluest Eye*. The coded allusion to the story of this raped classical goddess in the context of civil rights activism is one further means by which Morrison draws attention to the violation of women and their rights during this process. Furthermore, the allusion to archetypal rape is an important factor in Morrison's engagement with myths about America's discovery and colonization, and of the conventional use of rape as a trope to configure those historical processes. Through Cosey's creation of an empire on the very coast explored by conquistadors such as Ponce de Léon and De Soto, Morrison brings to mind the European conquest of that region. Cosey's relationship with the child-bride Heed can be understood as a parodic version of allegorical narratives that represent pre-European America as "virgin land," as an innocent virgin "taken" by a powerful conqueror.

The widespread invocation of ancient Rome in this novel also merits attention; it extends far beyond the fact that Romen is called "Romen." Streets in the town of Silk have "epic movie names," including one called "Gladiator" (40, 86), and the fact that the young protagonist is referred to by his family name, "the Gibbons boy" (24), connotes Edmund Gibbon's *Decline and Fall of the Roman Empire* (1776–89). Morrison thereby plays with the popular analogy between America and Rome. Through Cosey's failed empire, Morrison destabilizes the history of American imperialism, while through Romen's belief that he will imminently "become the Romen he always knew he was: chiselled, dangerous, loose" (46), and through the verisimilitude of Cosey's portrait, the author mocks the pertinacity of the classical heroic tradition in dominant American culture. The resort's founder is a flawed and fallen version of the "representative men," the heroic American archetypes whom Ralph Waldo Emerson celebrated in his lectures modeled on Plutarch's *Lives*.

L (and by extension Morrison) is keenly attuned to the human predilection for allegory and for dramatic self-presentation. "*The world is such a showpiece,*" she observes. "*Maybe that's why folks try to outdo it, put everything they feel onstage just to prove they can think things up too*" (63; original italics). In the prologue she imagines Heed and Christine as actors in a kind of Senecan or early modern revenge tragedy: "*one vomiting on the steps still holding the knife that cut the throat of the one that fed her the poison*" (9–10; original italics). Morrison frequently bestows an element of caricature, of allegorical figures in a morality play, on the characters in this novel – it could even be read as the satyr/satire play following the tragic trilogy that precedes it, as was the convention in classical theater. By calling her last chapter "Phantom" the author suggests not just the posthumous influence that Cosey exerts, but also the idea that he was never quite real. Like the notion of a heroic, omnipotent America, as Christine and Heed realize too late, "He made himself up," but "we must have helped" (189).

Heed's assessment of Cosey is crucial to the meaning of the novel as a whole: "He was everywhere. And nowhere" (189). Morrison implies that a range of ideologies – American exceptionalism, racial categorization and discrimination, class distinction and discrimination, patriarchy – are at once flimsily constructed and forces to be reckoned with. The strands of the story are unified by her interest in "the ability of power to satisfy its whims and ignore the consequences" (*L* xi) and by the search for strategies to avoid "girlish submission" (xii). Her moving words on the resources available to her during her own upbringing – "a feisty mother, a supportive father and insatiable reading habits" – illuminate the protection that Christine, Heed, and June must grow up without. Her reflection on the weapons that have enabled her own survival and success – "defiance, exit, knowledge; not solitude, but other people; not silence, but speech" (xi) – constitutes an insight to which most of the betrayed and betraying characters in *Love* come too late. The "hum" with which L ends the novel perfectly expresses the mood of ambivalence about the future (202); its sound resonates as an equivocal "hmmm."

A Mercy (2008)

A Mercy is set in colonial America: in the New England, Maryland, and Virginia of the late seventeenth century. Its central action – the journey undertaken by a young black enslaved woman, Florens, to find the blacksmith whom she loves and who can cure her dying mistress – takes place in May of 1690. To read *A Mercy* is to see colonial American in dramatically new light. Above all, it is to hear different voices: to listen to what slaves of both African descent and Native identity have to say, to confront the experiences of a working-class English woman who emigrated to marry an unknown homesteader, of a free African economically self-sufficient blacksmith, or of white indentured laborers. In this depiction of what the author has called "America before it was America,"[23] of the multicultural nature of this territory before monocultural narratives of nationhood were imposed upon it, we encounter stories that are not new, but that have been silenced or "disremembered" until now.

The novel's opening paragraph plunges the reader into the panic of uncertainty, indeterminacy, and the not-yet-understood. The compelling voice sets up a host of unanswered questions from the outset: who is speaking, and to whom, and what has he or she "done"? "One question is who is responsible? Another is can you read?" (*AM* 1); is this a book about moral agency, about literacy, and about their connectedness? Who or what is "a minha mãe"? In the second paragraph we learn that the speaker is a girl named Florens, that "a minha mãe" is her mother (the phrase means "my mother" in Portuguese), that in 1690 Florens is dispatched on a mission to find the person her narrative addresses, and that she sets off in her master's boots with a letter that she knows how to read, although she has not yet done so (2).

By paying close attention to Florens's words, here and in the subsequent five first-person monologues, as well as to the alternating six sections written in a third-person narrative voice (sometimes omniscient and sometimes limited), we are able to make sense of the central plot and its context. Florens, it transpires, is the daughter of an enslaved Angolan woman and a laborer of undefined identity who was ordered to "mate" with her (163). The girl is born and raised on a Maryland tobacco plantation owned by a Portuguese Roman Catholic gentleman named D'Ortega. She is given away in 1682, at the age of "seven or eight" (3), to the Anglo-Dutch Protestant farmer and trader Jacob Vaark, partly as a debt repayment and partly at her own mother's behest. Florens is delivered to Vaark's New England homestead, a smallholding worked by his wife, Rebekka, and her unpaid workers, the Native Lina, the foundling Sorrow, and the laborers leased from a neighboring farm, Willard and Scully.

The willingness of the formerly upstanding Vaark to accept the girl is, from her mother's perspective, the act of "mercy" to which the novel's title refers (164–5). Yet it is from this moment on that Vaark abandons his principles: he invests in the slave-dependent economy of the sugar plantations of Barbados and, with the help of the blacksmith, builds himself an unnecessarily grand house to rival D'Ortega's. In a manner that recalls a medieval morality tale, Vaark dies from smallpox precisely as his new mansion is finished. When Rebekka contracts the disease, Florens is sent to bring back the blacksmith (the love of her life), because he had previously cured Sorrow of the same condition. Florens does find the blacksmith, he does return, and Rebekka does survive the disease. But both on her journey and at the blacksmith's house, the girl undergoes trials she could not have foreseen. First, in a hamlet where she seeks refuge overnight, she is accused of being "the Black Man's minion" (111), an agent for the devil, by Separatists who have had no or few previous encounters with an "Afric" (109). Second, at the blacksmith's home, out of jealousy and rage at rejection, she attacks both the blacksmith's ward, a little boy, Malaik, and then the blacksmith himself. These experiences leave her forever changed.

Within this framework, in prose that is in a constant palimpsestic relationship with texts that precede it – the Bible; the canonical histories and literary works about colonial America; the slave narratives; the writings of Milton, of Blake, and of Wordsworth, to name but a few – Morrison asks questions that are as much about the present moment, the post 9/11 world, for example, as they are about the past. Can we, as writers and as readers, "shape the world," for example? Or is the truth that "the world shapes us" (9)? What does it mean for women to exist in a world controlled by men? By what means can those who are controlled and oppressed escape oppression and exert control? Beneath and alongside the dominant cultural mythology, what are the real implications of the relationships between race and ethnicity, social and economic class, gender and power, in America, and in the network that includes Europe, West Africa, and the Caribbean to which it is inextricably linked? How can we navigate the interconnectedness of freedom, free will, wrongdoing, and evil? What kind of man locates his self-worth in prosperity achieved through slavery? What kind of mother begs for her daughter to be taken from her? What kind of lover attacks the object of her desire? And where is salvation, where is the divine, in all of this?

Florens's "telling" (like the map on the novel's frontispiece, in which native names are written by European hand) is a hybrid text. It is a Portuguese-inflected pidgin English that only colonialism and the transatlantic slave trade could have produced. The non-Anglo nature of her language works to counter Anglocentric dominance in the canonical narratives of early America. It testifies both to her oppression, and, through the fact that it is a written as well as a spoken account, to the literacy wherein lies the potential for her freedom and escape.

It is only when we reach Florens's sixth and final monologue that we realize that she has written – or is writing – her story, her "confession," on the floors and the walls of Vaark's house (1). Much of *A Mercy* is more mythical and allegorical than it is documentary or socially realist, and this is particularly true of the sections she speaks/writes. The girl's voice gains much of its resonance and power from the fact that she speaks consistently in the present tense. The distinction between making the journey and writing about it disappears after her first narration, so that the act of writing about the quest becomes the quest itself, and vice versa. Through this fusion Morrison partakes of the ancient Greek concept of *logos*, meaning both "the word" and "the way," which is of such central importance in St John's Gospel. Through emphasizing the word "way" throughout the text, she explores the relationship between literacy, freedom, and power that is so central in the slave narratives.

Florens gives us her alternative Gospel, modified to the realities of enslaved life, and one that would make an excellent subtitle or epigraph to the text as a whole: "The beginning begins with the shoes" (*AM* 2). Throughout the text she is distinctive both for her predilection for shoes and for her way with words; these are her means to survival. The journey that she makes, the story that she tells, and the text that she writes combine to rewrite one of America's defining patriarchal paradigms: that of the traveling male hero (either white or black). At the 2008 Charleston reading of the novel, Morrison spoke of the significance of Florens's undertaking this mission with "no protection, no companion" (104): "Most females are sitting somewhere, in a house. I wanted this one to be in danger."

The novel's second section relates a very different journey: that of Vaark from his northern homestead, Milton, to Jublio, D'Ortega's plantation in Maryland. Here the author adopts a third-person narrative voice that privileges Vaark's perspective, revealing his contempt for the self-indulgent D'Ortega, for Catholicism, and for the corrupt slave economy of the plantation. The account begins in the realm of the epic or mythological, recalling and rewriting both the discovery narratives and Genesis: an as-yet unnamed man walks ashore in the Chesapeake Bay and travels by horseback through a "world" that is "new, almost alarming in rawness and temptation" (*AM* 10). This man can read and write; we learn his name from his signing to hire the horse, "Jacob Vaark" (8), and we learn that despite his own poverty growing up as an orphan in London, his literacy had enabled him to be signed up by the "[Virginia] Company" (31).

As he rides across Virginia, Vaark observes to himself that although it is "1682," this region is "still a mess," characterized by "lawless laws" that "authoriz[ed] chaos in defense of order" (*AM* 8–9). Feeling content to have escaped to inherited land in New England, his recollection of the "people's war" (Bacon's Rebellion of 1676), a class-driven rebellion in which "blacks, natives, white, mulattoes – freedmen, slaves and indentured" "had waged war against local gentry" (8), is indicative of Morrison's concern with class-based injustice and conflict in this novel. As Vaark dines and tours the plantation with D'Ortega, the narrative shifts a gear into a more psychologically realized, less mythical realm. There is much bitter humor in the depictions of the conversations about the loss of D'Ortega's "cargo" (14) or the relationships between Angola, Portugal, Maryland, and England. Vaark is physically repelled by his direct encounter with "the intimacy of slave bodies" that he encounters at Jublio (33) and suspects (correctly, as it transpires) that their owner indulges his sexual appetite with the cook, Floren's mother. His motives for succumbing to the woman's offering of her daughter are apparently unselfish and morally commendable: first, he wants more help for his wife on the farm, and, second, an orphan himself, he instinctively wishes to rescue "waifs and whelps" (30).

We go on to witness Vaark's moral collapse, however – a downfall of which the boastful, amoral promoter of the Barbadian slave/sugar/rum economy, Peter Downes, is the catalyst. Jacob's solitary walk out to the beach and his washing of "the faint trace of coon's blood" in the waves symbolize his conversion to a conscienceless pursuit of slave-dependent wealth (33). As several critics have observed, his new "dream," of a "grand house of many rooms rising on a hill above the fog" (69), stands in ironic counterpoint to St Paul's vision of God's kingdom and John Winthrop's iconic vision of a "city on a hill."

Through Rebekka, the mail order bride who welcomes escape from the poverty, stench, and ubiquitous violence of her London life, we encounter the author's first ever fictional representation of England. Morrison's picture completely subverts WASP Anglophilia, and through the specific experience of this woman she explores a sentiment common to millions of immigrants to the American continent: "America. Whatever the danger, how could it possibly be worse?" (76). Through a chapter devoted to Rebekka's sickbed meditation, in which her "thoughts bled into one another" (70), we discover that though she loved and respected Jacob, this lonely character has never recovered from the deaths of her three infant sons and from the subsequent loss of her firstborn, her daughter Patrician.

Through Rebekka's feverish hallucinations of the "exiled, thrown-away" women who accompanied her in steerage on the passage from London to New England (80), the author reconfigures her oeuvrewide thematic investment in the validity and resourcefulness of marginalized women. Despite the physical horrors of this crossing, one that functions in some ways as a whitened version of the Middle Passage, these "women of and for men" make the most of "the blank where a past did not haunt nor a future beckon" and of their temporary freedom from patriarchy (83). Through Rebekka's recollections of conversations with Lina and Jacob, and through drawing analogies between her own situation to that of Adam and Eve and Job, Morrison explores the troubled and troubling nature of the relationship between individual human suffering and divine presence, at the same time subverting or complicating the biblical archetypes on whom Rebekka muses. It is ironic that at the novel's end, once adopting the strictures of the Anabaptist faith to which her recovery from the smallpox converts her, she becomes insular, self-protective, and disregarding of the women in her care.

In exploring Rebekka's relationship with Lina, Morrison demonstrates that despite all they have in common through womanhood, there is a microhierarchy within the homestead in which Mistress Rebekka (thanks to her whiteness and Englishness) enjoys superior status. Like her fellow enslaved women at Milton, meanwhile, Lina has learned to survive with "no protection" (164). This character's traumatic past explains her intense "mother hunger" and her jealous protectiveness of Florens (61). Her maintaining of traditional skills and social practices makes her in many ways superior to the destructive, cowardly "Europes" who have colonized her land. Lina's "self-invention" (48), the fact that she "cobbled together" a new, hybridized identity and thereby "found … a way to be in the world" (46), evinces Morrison's conviction that the modern condition and modernist response to it – that of dislocation and reformation – began with the colonial project and slavery. Lina knows, however, that if Rebekka were to die, she and her coslaves, "three unmastered women" with neither power nor rights, would become "wild game for anyone" (56).

Despite the fact that Sorrow's motherhood makes her "Complete" by the novel's end (*AM* 132), she is in many ways the most fully dispossessed member of this novel's cast. She is certainly its most ambiguous: rescued from a shipwreck by a sawyer and his wife, she has indefinable "woolly hair" that is "the color of a setting sun" (49), which suggests a mixed, racial heritage.[24] Her suffering, including multiple sexual abuses, has caused her psyche to split into two, and the fact that she and "Twin" observe in baffled amazement the consensual lovemaking of Florens and the blacksmith consolidates Morrison's thematic concern with sexual violence. The author extends this concern to sexual abuse of men: as a child, the twenty-two-year-old Scully was subject to prolonged abuse by "an Anglican curate" (151). Through both Scully and Willard, with whom the former is in a homosexual relationship, Morrison explores, first, the prenational parity between unpaid workers of different races, and, second, the comparatively easy rise up the social scale that white men enjoyed. At the novel's end Rebekka plans to sell Florens, subjects Sorrow to physical violence, and imposes new restrictions on Lina, but she "relied on" the two white men so much that she "paid them" (152).

The ambivalent figure of the African blacksmith, who has affinities both with the classical Vulcan and with Mulciber in Milton's *Paradise Lost* and

Ovid's *Metamorphoses*, also appears to distinguish between the women of various ethnicities and the white men; he addresses Willard as "Mr Bond" (148). He shows compassion in taking Malaik into his care, yet his condemnation and dismissal of Florens, when he discovers she has injured the boy, are immediate and absolute. He does not ask for her side of the story, and that may be why she chooses to write it. We never know whether she killed or simply injured him in her attack, and so whether her text is addressed to him beyond or before the grave.

It is possible that the snake heads ending in flowers that the blacksmith forges for Jacob's gate are a tribute to Florens, whose name is the Latin present participle meaning both "flowering" and "flourishing." Florens's declaration, "I am become wilderness but I am also Florens. In full," suggests that she has gone wild but is also flourishing (159). She has survived her epic journey through "pathless night" (3), including not being raped, to her surprise, by a group of Native boys on horseback. She has also survived being scrutinized by the Separatists. In this scene, which exists in complex dialogue with *The Scarlet Letter,* Arthur Miller's *The Crucible*, and *Paradise Lost*, Morrison engages the age-old association between blackness and evil. The Elders' inspection, furthermore, anticipates the inspection of slave bodies prior to sale, while their idea of a contained, external "evil" allegorically connotes the Bush administration's rhetoric of "the axis of evil" in the wake of 9/11. Perhaps the only redeeming aspect of this encounter is the courage of Daughter Jane, who "risks all" to help Florens escape (158) and whose affirmative answer to Florens's question "Are you a demon?" is a moment of profoundly comic seriousness (113). The blacksmith's subsequent choosing Malaik over Florens recalls both her perceived rejection by her mother in favor of her brother and the unnamed Separatist girl's hysterical ostracism. "Both times are full of danger and I am expel" (134), she thinks, and a refusal to countenance a third "expel" motivates her attack (135).

Once Florens has returned to Milton, she abandons traveling and "decide[s] for stillness" (41). Her choice of the word "stillness" to imply the stationary creativity of writing resonates in Morrison's use of the same word in her anti-censorship essay "Peril" (2009), where she equates it with the "art" that is a powerful response to "chaos" (*BTB* 3). Recalling Morrison's central metaphor in "Home," the text and the house become one through Florens's writing on the walls and the floors, and through the ash to which the fire gives rise, the words disperse throughout the world. The failure of communication between mother and child, Florens's misunderstanding of her mother's action, becomes painfully central in the final paragraph. Having addressed her whole narrative thus far to the illiterate blacksmith, she directs her final sentence and that one only, to her mother.

The voice of Florens's mother (we never learn her name), speaking for the first time, is the voice that closes the book. Addressing her words to an absent Florens, she explains that her motivation for giving her to Vaark was the certainty that she would be raped and expresses her belief in literacy as defense. In one present tense paragraph and one past, the mother recalls her life in Africa and her capture. This is notable for being Morrison's first depiction of action on the African continent and for its challenge to the oversimplified polarization between black victimhood and white oppression or to a straight equation between race and slavery: "The men guarding we and selling we are black" (162). As she describes the process of her enslavement, the black-washing of her specific identity into a commodifed, universalized blackness is particularly striking: "I was negrita. ... Language, dress, gods, dance, habits, decoration, song – all of it cooked together in the color of my skin" (163). In her penultimate paragraph, the repeated word "dominion" speaks to power and mastery in a number of contexts, both seventeenth-century and contemporary (165): of the political dominion characterizing colonization and slavery, of the power imbalance in gender relations, of the exercising of sexual dominion or violent domination, and of mastery of the self, or self-determination. The mother's implication that Florens's self-surrender to the blacksmith is "a wicked thing" might provoke the daughter if she were to hear it, but although the novel ends on a note of heartfelt pleading to be heard, the speaker's words appear to join Florens's dispersed text, falling "out in the world" (159), where the only guaranteed audience is Morrison's reader.

Other Creative Work

"Recitatif" (1983)

Morrison's only published short story (to date) first appeared in the 1983 collection *Confirmation: An Anthology of African-American Women*, edited by Amiri and Amina Baraka, which is now out of print. It has been reanthologized several times, for example, in the 7th edition of the *Norton Anthology of American Literature* (2007), and is also available online.

The story is narrated in the first person by Twyla, a woman who looks back on the four months she spent in a children's home or "shelter" when she was eight years old (*R* 243). She remembers the friend she made there, Roberta, and recalls the times they have run into each other since then. They both still live in the Newburgh/Annandale region of New York State, and their chance meetings have occurred over the course of the 1950s and 1960s, during the civil rights advances (such as school integration) that those years involved.

The story anticipates *Paradise* in two key ways: in its focus on girls who exist on the periphery of society and in its configurations of racial identity. Twyla tells us that Roberta is "from a whole other race" (*R* 243), yet throughout the story while Morrison marks the pair as racially different from each other, she never confirms which girl is white and which is black. Both in *Playing in the Dark* and in a 1992 interview, the author draws attention to her technique, the "removal of all racial codes," in this story (*PiD* xiii; *DC* 74–5). But the story is also about class and its interactions with race and gender (both women rise up the social scale through marriage) and about the nature of memory and of shame (Twyla cannot remember her exact role in the persecution of Maggie, the mute domestic worker in the children's home). The often-ignored presence of Maggie makes disability, and the ways both characters and readers interpret it, a central theme in the story.[25]

District Storyville (1982)

In the early 1980s Morrison wrote the lyrics, to music by Sidney Bechet, for a musical called *District Storyville* which was based on the 1962 ballet of the same title choreographed by Donald McKayle. As Abena Busia writes in her useful overview of the major shorter works, Storyville, the red-light district of New Orleans, "was the only place in the United States where prostitution was legal. ... The musical is a tribute, a portrait of a district through the people who lived in it."[26] Busia notes that "although the version to Bechet's music has not been recorded, those words were later set to original music by André Previn and can be found on his album *Honey and Rue*," and that "the musical itself has been performed in workshop only once, at the Michael Bennett Studios on Broadway in the summer of 1982" (Busia 102).

Dreaming Emmett

Although Morrison completed this play while in her professorial post at SUNY Albany, which she took up in 1984, she has said that she first conceived of it in 1983 (*TG* 219). A response to the notorious murder of the fourteen-year-old Chicago-born black youth Emmett Till, who was lynched by two white men in Money, Mississippi, in August 1955, the play was produced at the Capital Repertory Theater in Albany in January 1986. It was commissioned by the New York State Writer's Institute, was directed by Gilbert Moses, and won the New York State Governor's Award.

In *Song of Solomon* the murder of Till is a defining moment for Guitar, and it is also referenced in *Love*. In a 1995 interview, Morrison speaks briefly of Till and of her play to Cecil Brown: "That kid tore the place up," she says. "The whole play was about what was on his mind" (*DC* 124). The play text is officially unavailable, so what follows is a brief summary of the analyses by Busia (who has read a copy of the working script preserved by a stage manager) and by Margaret Croyden, whose interview with Morrison at the time of the production is reprinted in the Taylor-Guthrie collection. Busia describes the plot as follows:

> A young Black man appears on stage and begins to direct a film about "How I spent my summer, 1955," and summoning up his holiday friends, begins to recreate the summer as he would have had it. But the characters he summons, Black and white, resist his reverie, because they have changed, and because if they enter into his dream, as he is dead and they alive, they are subject to indictment. (Busia 105)

The critic explains that in this nonnaturalistic, allegorical drama, in which the actors sometimes wear masks, the titular word "dreaming" applies both to the characters who dream of Emmett and to the Emmett-like character who dreams his memories. The Emmett figure in Morrison's play is representative of "the plight of contemporary black urban youth" (*TG* 220). As the author told Croyden, "There are these young men getting shot all over the country today, not because they were stealing but because they're black" (*TG* 220). Both the themes and the dramatic technique of the play will resonate with anyone familiar with Morrison's novels: she uses a disrupted chronology to explore the nature of memory, of vengeance, of sexual desire, and of the incendiary effects of the hint of interracial sexual relations.

Margaret Garner

Margaret Garner was the slave woman from Kentucky whose attack on her own children inspired Morrison's writing of the novel *Beloved*. The Michigan Opera Theatre, Detroit, saw the world premiere of the opera, *Margaret Garner*, for which Morrison wrote the libretto to a musical score by Richard Danielpour, on May 7, 2005. This first production (a collaboration between Michigan Opera Theatre, Cincinnati Opera, and the Opera Company of Philadelphia) played for three nights in Cincinnati in July 2005 and in Philadelphia in February 2006. To date there have been three further productions of the opera: Opera Carolina's, which played in Charlotte, North Carolina, in April 2006; New York City Opera's, which played at the Lincoln Center's New York State Theater in September 2006; and a second Michigan Opera production, staged in Detroit in October 2008 and Chicago in November the same year. Although the libretto cannot comprise the literary sophistication of any of Morrison's novels, the opera project as a whole is a fascinating forum for the consideration of many vintage Morrisonian themes: the relationship between the personal and the public or political, between memory and history, between literature and music, and between political and aesthetic imperatives.

The opera is in two acts, has two choruses, and runs to nearly three hours. The plot, in brief summary, is as follows: in northern Kentucky, in 1856, a white man named Edward Gaines assumes ownership of Maplewood Plantation and its slaves on the death of his brother. Gaines compels the field slave Margaret Garner to become a house slave, and he sexually assaults her at the end of the first act. In the second act, Robert, Margaret's husband, and Margaret escape across the river to the free state of Ohio, but not before Robert has killed the overseer who tries to prevent the escape. When the escapees are discovered, Gaines orders the lynching of Robert; on the point of her recapture, Margaret murders both her children. Gaines puts Margaret on trial for the theft and destruction of his property (crucially, not for murder, a charge that would have acknowledged the humanity and rights of slaves). When the judge sentences Margaret to death, Gaines's daughter begs her father to seek a stay of execution, but Margaret deliberately hangs herself just as this is granted.

As Busia notes, Morrison's libretto changes the historical record in some key ways, for example, in changing the year of Margaret's escape and trial from 1856 to 1861. There has been critical controversy about the political implications of other changes made to the facts – for example, that the real Robert Garner escaped, remarried, and raised the surviving members of his family is obscured by his lynching in the opera. While it is probably fair to say that this work is not a masterpiece, it is nonetheless significant as a high-cultural recognition of a story that (though notorious in the abolition era) was little known in the pre-*Beloved* decades of the twentieth century, and for its placing the idiom of African-American vernacular at center stage.

Desdemona

The world premiere of *Desdemona* (formerly entitled "The Desdemona Project") took place on 15 May 2011 at Theatre Akzent in Vienna. This production, a counterpoint to Shakespeare's *Othello*, is a collaboration between Morrison (who wrote the spoken text), the Malian singer-songwriter Rokia Traoré (who wrote the songs and to date has performed them, as Barbary), and the theater director Peter Sellars, to whose 2009 production of Shakespeare's *Othello* (at the Public Theater in New York City) *Desdemona* is in many ways a sequel. During 2011, the show played in order of performance Brussels, Paris, New York, Berlin, and Berkeley, California, and, as I write this book, is scheduled for London in July 2012.

Desdemona takes its inspiration from the famous "Willow song" scene in Shakespeare's play, in which the fearful Desdemona talks to Emilia of her mother's maid, Barbary (IV.3.24–31). Interpolating from these lines that this remembered Barbary was both an African slave and Desdemona's childhood nurse, the Morrison/Sellars/Traoré collaboration stages a conversation from beyond the grave between these two women. In the Paris performance (Théâtre des Amandiers, October 2011), Desdemona was played by a white actress, Tina Benko. Traoré (who is black) as Barbary sang songs that were mostly in Bambara (the predominant language of Mali), and sometimes in French. Sometimes Barbary held center stage, accompanying herself on the guitar, and at others Desdemona spoke her own text as a "voice-over" to Traoré's music. The only other people on the stage were three black women who made up the chorus of vocalists/dancers and two black men playing traditional West African instruments.

The English text is structured on a series of remembered dialogues that epitomize key relationships: Desdemona's with her mother, Desdemona's with Othello, Desdemona's with Emilia, and Desdemona's with Barbary. The recreated stories engage with and extend some of the more controversial aspects of Sellars's 2009 *Othello*, such as the suggestion that Emilia and Othello had a sexual relationship. Throughout, he and Morrison implicitly reference contemporary politics and the post-9/11 world. Morrison's text, in addition, picks up on and reformulates key themes of her novelistic oeuvre: the significance of naming and misnaming, the female propensity to self-sabotage through excessive passion, the oppression of women by men, the vulnerability of "orphans," the violence of violence and of political subjugation, and the elusive nature of "safety" and of "home."

Books for Children

At the time of this book's going to press, Morrison has published eight storybooks for children that she co-authored with her now-late son, Slade Morrison. The first of these was *The Big Box* (1999), and the most recent (and last to be published in Slade's lifetime) was *Little Cloud and Lady Wind* (2010). Many of these works for children challenge conventional power dynamics and subvert the platitudinous kinds of language with which adults exert control over their young. *The Big Box,* for example, describes three children who are kept locked up in a "big brown box" (np) and who argue with adults about the nature of real freedom. The trio that has attracted the most scholarly attention is the fascinating *Who's Got Game?* series, the three revisions of Aesop's fables (*The Ant or the Grasshopper?*, 2003; *The Lion or the Mouse?*, 2004; and *Poppy or the*

Snake?, 2004), which were illustrated by Pascale Lemaître and published by Scribner. In 2004 Morrison published a history book for children, *Remember: The Journey to School Integration,* in which she gives voice to the people in the iconographic photos of this era.

Nonfiction

Although there is less of it, Morrison's nonfiction is every bit as groundbreaking, wide-ranging, challenging, and enduring as her fiction. One of the privileges of writing this book is the opportunity to give a long-overdue emphasis to the significance of this nonfictional corpus. Her long and short essays, speeches, interviews, public letters, forewords to her own work, and so on, have shored up her position as more than "just" a novelist. They compel acknowledgment of Morrison's rightful place as a serious player in intellectual history; as a key figure in modern thought; as a writer, thinker, and commentator on literature, politics, and society, whose significance extends far beyond the parameters of the genre in which she excels.

Morrison's nonfictional writings were not published in any collected form until 2008, when *What Moves at the Margin: Selected Non-Fiction* (edited by Carolyn Denard) made its very welcome appearance. With its wonderfully punning title taken from Morrison's Nobel acceptance speech, this anthology is invaluable for presenting many of Morrison's otherwise hard-to-track-down writings in one place. Nearly all of the key short pieces are here, although it is important to be aware that there are also several notable absences. Key essays that are seminal but omitted (presumably because of copyright restrictions) are "Unspeakable Things Unspoken" (1989); "City Limits, Village Values" (1981); and "Home" (1997). Additionally, Morrison's recently published forewords to her novels (in the Vintage editions from 2003 onward) have become a significant component of the nonfiction corpus. To date there are seven forewords in all, prefacing the novels from *The Bluest Eye* to *Love,* with the exception of *Paradise.* These prefatory pieces are profoundly valuable but should not be approached uncritically.

This author has also been a generous and prolific interviewer throughout her career, although as she herself reflects after her meeting with Gloria Naylor in 1985, she prefers the term and the concept of "conversation" to that of "interview" (*TG* 215). Most of these pieces (from 1974 to 2005) have been collected into two indispensable volumes: *Conversations with Toni Morrison,* edited by Danille Taylor-Guthrie (1994), and *Toni Morrison: Conversations,* edited by Carolyn Denard (2008). There are also many public talks, readings, and interviews available on youtube or archived on the NPR and BBC Web sites.

Morrison on Her Own Life and Work

Toni Morrison has consistently stated that she will never write a formal autobiography; "I can't remember anything," she claimed, somewhat mischievously, in Paris in 2010. What she has revealed about her life in her nonfictional short pieces and interviews is therefore all the more valuable. Her analyses of herself should, of course, be read for what they are – as acts of self-fashioning, as stylized performances rather than revelations of truth – but they are no less informative for that. Her 1976 article "A Slow Walk of Trees" is a fascinating reflection on the complex and conflicting perspectives of each of her maternal grandparents and her own parents, and on the history of race relations and the nature of black advancement in the United States. The piece that follows it in *What Moves at the Margin*, "She and Me," was published nearly thirty years later, but its short anecdote about her job as a cleaner for a white woman, when aged twelve, gives profound insight into her relationship with her father and her attitude to her life's work.

The autobiographical vignettes in the author's recent forewords, furthermore, combine to form a much fuller picture of her childhood, family relationships, and adult life than her interviews or previous essays have revealed. To arrange the information they contain in chronological order creates a fascinating contrapuntal relationship between the stages of her life and the composition/publication sequence of the novels themselves. The earliest memory she recalls, for example, is in the foreword to *Jazz*, which relates the scintillating encounter between her preschool self and her mother's keepsakes from the 1920s, while the foreword to *Tar Baby* includes present-tense recollections of her grandmother's life and dying (*TB* xii). The forewords also illuminate what Morrison disarmingly calls "the fuzzy area between autobiography and fiction" (*SoS* ix). She articulates there her "inspiration" for each novel – that the "origin" of *The Bluest Eye*, for example, "lay in a conversation [she] had with a childhood friend" who wanted blue eyes (*BE* np). In the foreword to *Sula* she makes an elliptical reference to the real woman called "Hannah Peace," who, as she recalls in the essay "The Site of Memory" (1987), "was a little bit of an outlaw" (*WMM* 74). And the foreword to *Love* recalls a twelve-year-old classmate who was being abused sexually by her own father. Such revelations exemplify the way Morrison's fiction embodies what she has called "the inwardness of the outside," of the public or political nature of the "personal" (*H*12).

Morrison has written significant analyses of her own fiction. It could be argued that while she herself carved out the space for her own writing through her editing of others and her early nonfictional declarations about black literature and culture, she has also taught us how to read her own texts. At the same time, you should view her efforts to control the reception of her work as exactly that, and not mistake them for "truth." Her summaries of the thematic concerns of each novel in its foreword are in many ways regrettable, in that they negate her previous insistence on active reading, and on fruitful collaboration between reader and writer (for example, in the important 1984 essay "Rootedness"). Paradoxically enough, of greater value than the forewords' thematic summaries are the passages in which Morrison discusses her authorial struggles and regrets. Such revelations – which include her dissatisfaction with some aspects of *The Bluest Eye* (*BE* np) or the abandoned initial first sentence to *Jazz* (*J* ix) – serve to lay bare the painstaking nature of her creative process and to intensify the attention we pay to the innumerable narrative dilemmas she has faced.

Among the qualities of "black literature" that Morrison delineates in "Rootedness," her emphasis there on the "presence of an ancestor" (by which she implies both the familial and the literary kind) prepares the ground for the later essay, "The Site of Memory" (*WMM* 61). In the latter she positions her own writing in relation to both her own personal memories and black cultural or political memory as articulated in the slave narratives. She herself mines the influences that her literary and biological forebears have had on her life, observing that the slave narratives are characterized by an absence of "interior life" and explaining "the wish to extend, fill in and complement" those narratives that discussed previously in relation to *Beloved* (*WMM* 70, 77). Together with her manifesto about "rebuilding" and "transforming" the "racial house" in the essay "Home," these statements are Morrison's most explicit self-descriptors of her project (*H* 5).

You should not approach Morrison's interviews with the expectation of finding consistency in the positions she adopts. The fact that she inevitably contradicts herself in four decades of discussion about her own life and writing, on the writing of others, on American culture and society, and on the interconnectedness of all of these – is a useful caveat about relying too strongly on the concept of authorial intention, or about our surrendering of our own power and responsibilities to her views. The interviews need no explication; particularly enlightening ones in the Taylor-Guthrie collection are those with Robert Stepto (1976), with Charles Ruas (1981), with Nellie McKay (1983), with Gloria Naylor (1985), with Bill Moyers (1989), and with Betty Fussell (1992). In the Denard *Conversations* collection, highlights are an early one with Jessica Harris (1976), the interview article entitled "A Bench by the Road" (1988), with Salman Rushdie (1992), with Ellissa Schappell (1992), two interviews with Michael Silverblatt (1998 and 2004), and a pivotal one with Denard herself, on the subject "Modernism and the American South," given in 1998. Of the uncollected interviews, Hilton Als's *New Yorker* profile of 2003 is particularly illuminating (*GiA*).

Literary Criticism

Morrison's major pieces of literary critical scholarship are the 1989 essay "Unspeakable Things Unspoken: The Afro-American Presence in American Literature" and *Playing in the Dark: Whiteness and the Literary Imagination*, which is a ninety-page extended essay published in 1992. The title "Unspeakable Things Unspoken" recalls the voices that Stamp Paid hears in *Beloved*, "unspeakable thoughts unspoken" (*B* 124). The essay addresses itself, first, to questions of canon formation. When revisited in the early decades of the twenty-first century, its assertions that Western culture is not "superior" now read as accepted fact, but their simultaneous necessity and forcefulness when originally uttered, at the height of the culture wars, should not be underestimated. Morrison pays tribute to scholars whose (then-recent) work challenged and unsettled Western cultural imperialism, such as Edward Said (to whose theory of "Orientalism" her own theory of "Africanism" in *Playing in the Dark* is clearly indebted) and Martin Bernal, whose examinations of "motive" in the "history of history" in his 1987 work *Black Athena*, she strongly applauds (*UTU* 7–8).

In the second part of the essay, Morrison moves from a discussion of problematic practice in critical approaches to "Afro-American literature" to a definition of her "unspeakable things unspoken": "the ways in which the presence of Afro-Americans has shaped the choice, the language, the structure – the meaning of so much American literature" (*UTU* 11). Here we see the seeds of her focus in *Playing in the Dark*. Her discussion of Ahab in *Moby-Dick*, and of Melville's "recognition of the moment in America when whiteness became ideology," was to become a catalyst in the still-burgeoning field of "whiteness studies" (*UTU* 15). The third part of her essay effects a fascinating close reading of the openings of her own first five novels, demonstrating the ways in which her work is "inseparable from a cultural specificity that is Afro-American" (*UTU* 19). She concludes by illuminating the high political stakes that the practice of literature entails: "As far as the future is concerned, when one writes, as critic or as author, all necks are on the line" (*UTU* 34).

Besides Morrison's invaluable analysis of the slave narratives in "The Site of Memory," most of her critical analyses of African-American and African writing center on that of her more immediate forebears and contemporaries. *What Moves at the Margin* includes some fascinating tributes by Morrison from as early as 1972, when she published a review of Albert Murray's *South to a Very Old Place* (1971), in which she illuminates his emphasis on "home." In 1974 she commemorated the then-just-killed Henry Dumas through celebrating his poetry, *Play Ebony Play Ivory* (1974), and stories, *Ark of Bones* (1974); and in 1975 she published a paean to Gayl Jones's 1975 novel, *Corregidora*. The collection also reprints Morrison's 1987 eulogy for James Baldwin. Published in the *New York Times Book Review*, addressed in the first person to the just-deceased male author, it is a clear declaration of indebtedness to a literary ancestor: "You knew, didn't you, how I needed your language and the mind that formed it?" (*WMM* 93). More than ten years later, although it contains none of her explicit analysis, Morrison's editorial role in the Library of America's *James Baldwin: Collected Essays* (1998) is itself a form of literary criticism.

Morrison's debt to Baldwin is also expressed in her wonderful 1981 essay "City Limits, Village Values," a piece that should be better known than it is. Starting by recalling Baldwin's sense of alienation from Chartres Cathedral, Morrison argues that black writing is distinguished from white by its investment in a "hero who prefers the village and its tribal values to heroic loneliness and isolation" (*CL* 38). Her discussion here of Hughes, Bambara, Toomer, and others reiterates the importance of the "benevolent ancestor" (*CL* 39) for which she first argues "Rootedness" (1984). In that earlier essay she distinguishes between black autobiography, in which the writer aims to be "like the lives of the tribe ... both solitary and representative," and contemporary non-black autobiography, which, by contrast, demands, "look at me – alone – let me show you how I did it" (*WMM* 57).

Like all of Morrison's musings on other writers, her 1996 preface to Toni Cade Bambara's posthumously published collection *Deep Sightings and Rescue Missions* sheds light on the impulses and priorities of her own work while also serving as valuable criticism in its own right. This piece is a moving testimony to Morrison's disregard for the "art/politics fake debate" (*WMM* 88). In her long 2001 piece on *The Radiance of the King* (1954) Morrison praises its Guinean author, Camara Laye, for his not-dissimilar "blend of art and politics, freedom and responsibility" (*WMM* 128). Morrison's observations in the same essay that for non-African white authors, Africa "could be made to serve a wide variety of literary and/or ideological requirements" recalls her theory of American Africanism in *Playing in the Dark* (*WMM* 119).

The author's focus in *Playing* is on how "literary whiteness" and "literary blackness" are made, and on the "consequence of that construction" (*PiD* xiv). She investigates what she calls the "dark, abiding, signing Africanist presence" in canonical literary texts authored by white Americans (*PiD* 5). In the first of three chapters she identifies the persistence of a "willful critical blindness" (18), a refusal to discuss the presence and purpose of black characters in white texts, citing scholars' silence about those in Cather's *Sapphira and the Slave Girl* as a case in point. Her theory of "American Africanism" is that white American authors project their own personal concerns onto nonwhite characters, using them to perform a kind of "black surrogacy," as a vehicle for their own "fears and desires" (13; 17).

In the second chapter the author discusses works by Poe, Melville, Twain, and Faulkner as she explores "the presence of the unfree within the heart of the democratic experiment" (*PiD* 48). She cites Bernard Bailyn's account (in *Voyages to the West*, 1986) of one William Dunbar, a prototypical "Enlightened" Scottish settler in the Mississippi of the late eighteenth century. She argues that the romance genre is not "an evasion of history" but instead a "head-on encounter with very real, pressing historical forces and the contradictions inherent in them" (36). She also emphasizes the mutually constitutive and interdependent nature of slavery and freedom, of Africanism and "the rights of man" (38).

Her final chapter explores the nature and effects of the metaphorical nature of "race." Building on the work of James Snead, and with a precision invaluable to critics who wish to continue the type of close reading Morrison initiates in this book, she identifies "six linguistic strategies employed in fiction to engage the serious consequences of blacks" (*PiD* 67–9). In concluding her illuminations of "the transference to blackness of the power of illicit sexuality, chaos, madness, impropriety, anarchy, strangeness, and helpless, hapless desire" (81), she analyses two novels by Ernest Hemingway. It would be hard to overemphasize the enduring influence of Playing, first, for the ways in which it illuminates her own intellectual formation and concerns (which have influenced comparative scholarly approaches to her fiction), and, second, for the way in which "disrupting darkness," and the processes by which it is created, can be unnoticed no longer (91).

Morrison develops her reading of *Huckleberry Finn* in her introduction to the Oxford edition of the novel edited by Shelley Fisher Fishkin. Her insights about the novel and her skeptical engagement here with the 1950s analyses by Leslie Fiedler and Lionel Trilling have become central to scholarly debate about Twain. Her discussions of William Faulkner, meanwhile, though more scattered and less formalized than her work on Twain, have become influential in Faulkner studies and, of course, in the ever-burgeoning study of the relationship between the two authors that I discuss in Chapter 4.

Politics, Society, Language, and Literature

In 1992 Morrison edited and introduced an essay collection entitled *Race-ing Justice, En-gendering Power*. This work, as its subtitle states, addresses "Anita Hill, Clarence Thomas, and the Construction of Social Reality." Its focus is October 1991, when Anita Hill (an African-American attorney and professor) made allegations of sexual harassment against Clarence Thomas (a senior African-American judge) at the televised Senate hearings on the confirmation of Thomas as Supreme Court justice. Thomas was eventually confirmed to his position by fifty-two votes to forty-eight.[27] The star-studded cast of contributors to Morrison's volume discusses the complex interactions among language, representation, law, and politics in these events, which caused both tabloid sensation and outrage among the intelligentsia. Morrison's introductory essay, "Friday on the Potomac," is energized by her customary combination of political conviction and devastatingly witty irony. Her analysis of the way the discourse of race functioned paradoxically in these events, as a "powerfully destructive emptiness" (*RJEP* ix), draws an analogy between Man Friday, the accommodating, linguistically compromised savage in Defoe's 1719 novel *Robinson Crusoe* and the morally compromised Clarence Thomas. After her piercing critical analysis of that novel, Morrison pushes her point home in no uncertain terms. "Being rescued into an adversarial culture can carry a huge debt," she argues (*RJEP* xxvii). "One is obliged to cooperate in the misuse of figurative language, in the reinforcement of cliché, the erasure of difference, the jargon of justice, the evasion of logic, the denial of history, the crowning of patriarchy, [and] the inscription of hegemony" (*RJEP* xxviii–xxix).

Morrison's second collection of sociocritical essays, *Birth of a Nation'hood: Gaze, Script and Spectacle in the O. J. Simpson Case,* appeared in 1997. This project is co-edited with her Princeton colleague Claudia Brodsky Lacour, and its subject is the high-profile murder trial of the African-American football player O. J. Simpson in 1995.[28] In her introductory essay, "The Official Story: Dead Man Golfing," Morrison once again focuses on the ways in which the events were represented. She exposes how the "national narrative" about the O. J. Simpson case has relied on the stereotype of "black irrationality" (*BN* xiii), on "gargantuanism" (BN xiii), and on the "spectacle" of "the house at Rockingham awash in blood" (xxi). She argues that the narrative shares with D. W. Griffith's 1915 film *Birth of a Nation* "the old sham white supremacy forever wedded to and dependent upon faux black inferiority" (*BN* xvii).

Entirely different in purpose and tone, but of no less political import, is Morrison's magnificent Nobel Lecture, published as a small hardback by Knopf in 1994 and reprinted (without the acceptance speech section) in *What Moves at the Margin*.[29] The lecture is an exploration of the power of language, as a force for both good and bad, and of literature's transformative potential. It centers on the archetypal story of the wise but blind old woman who is asked by two young people whether the bird in their hands is alive or dead. Eventually the woman replies that she does not know, but that what she does know is that the bird "is in your hands" – in other words, "it is your responsibility" (*WMM* 198–9). Frustrated by the woman's silence, the young people go on to ask her a series of questions about the present and the past, and about their role and responsibilities in the world, until the woman testifies to their proficiency in language and to the power of their collaboration with her. In the acceptance speech itself, Morrison expresses her sense of being haunted by the "brilliance" of former laureates, of her faith in the future of literary creativity, and of her sense that her achievement was one that she shared with her "sisters" (*NL* 31, 32).

Morrison has continued her meditations on the power of language, on the political significance of intellectual activity and of art, in several pieces published since the Nobel. One striking example is "The Dancing Mind," her speech on acceptance of the National Book Foundation Medal in 1996. The speech is a tribute to "the peace" that is "the dance of an open mind when it engages another equally open one," exemplified by the "reading/writing world" (*WMM* 187). The author's words here both recall the reader/writer relationship she configures in *Jazz* and anticipate her 2009 essay, "Peril," with which she introduces the PEN anticensorship collection of essays by distinguished novelists, *Burn This Book*. "Peril," in its advocacy of "art" as a response to "chaos," speaks movingly to the post-9/11 world (*BTB* 3).

Finally, it is important to highlight the fact that since 1971, when she published an unequivocal critique of white middle-class feminism ("What the Black Woman Thinks about Women's Lib") in the *New York Times Magazine*, Morrison has continued to intervene in the cultural and political "moment" in short, pithy articles and public statements. Her much-quoted evaluation of Bill Clinton in 1998 and her public letter endorsing Barack Obama in January 2008 are just two examples of these; *What Moves at the Margin* contains several more. You should not forget, as well, that Morrison's intellectual patronage or curatorship of the arts, for example, in the Princeton Atelier program, or at the Louvre, where she was guest curator in 2006, also constitutes a social/political/aesthetic intervention of an important kind.[30]

Chapter 3

Contexts

Morrison and African-American History and Tradition

It is impossible to appreciate the depth and complexity of Toni Morrison's work without some knowledge of the depth and complexity of African-American history and tradition. Given that in the eyes of the world this author is one of *the* faces of black American culture, to argue that the ways she expresses and critiques that culture is at the heart of her fiction may sound like an empty truism. Moreover, the divisions of this chapter – between "African-American," "American," and "African" contexts – rely to some extent on false distinctions and falsify the vision of a novelist who eschews the simplistic "either/or" perspective in favor of the sophisticated "both . . . and." With this in mind, my hope is that the last section of this chapter, "Morrison, Transnational Perspectives, Modernism, and Postmodernism," resolves the limitations of the preceding categories: it demonstrates the author's central role in the intellectual movements of recent decades that transcend boundaries of national and racial identity. Nonetheless, as one of Morrison's greatest achievements is to combine universalism with a specific engagement with black experience, it is important to establish some of the particularities of African-American history, folk tradition, religion, music, literature, and art that have shaped her work and that she continues to shape.

Morrison has written of her "reliance for full comprehension on codes embedded in black culture" (*BE* np). In illuminating some of those "codes" and their presences in her novels, this chapter presents a brief chronological overview of the changing status of people of African descent in America, and of their always-evolving artistic forms. While Morrison's fiction is absolutely rooted in black traditions, it is of course never simply a mouthpiece or vehicle of propaganda promoting some vague notion of "black worth." While the author obviously participates in the ongoing African-American struggle for genuine emancipation and equality, her novels never blindly endorse the forms that that struggle has taken. Her approach to the Harlem Renaissance of the 1920s, for example, or to the Black Power movement of the 1960s is one of analysis and critical engagement rather than wholehearted celebration. She looks behind and beyond the prevailing myths of black history as well as white, perhaps no more so than in her attention to the experience of black women, in the positioning of women and girls at the center of her novels. Even in *Song of Solomon*, in which the protagonist, Milkman, is male, Morrison enacts through Pilate, through Ruth, through Corrie and Lena a specificity of engagement, a consideration of precise social circumstances and cultural pressures, that is characteristic of her oeuvre-wide concern with what African-American women have been doing, thinking, saying, and not saying over the last four centuries.

The last point to bear in mind when considering the interactions between African-American culture and Morrison's work is that she writes within a context of at least two simultaneous time frames: the time in which a novel is set and the time in which she is writing it. For example, *Beloved* is a book about slavery and its aftermath, about Kentucky and Ohio in the nineteenth century. But it is also about what it means to confront that subject in the 1980s, and, therefore, it is about the position and representation of African-Americans during the Republican presidency of Ronald Reagan. *Sula* is set primarily in the 1940s, yet in its foreword Morrison writes of her experience of "snatching liberty" and of "female friendship" at the time she wrote the novel: "in 1969, in Queens" (*S* xv). The productive friction between when the actions are set and when the author writes about them is one to which readers should always be alert. Since Morrison has been writing novels for more than forty years, she frequently now has a third time frame, the political culture at the time of a text's particular edition, in play. Her recent forewords to new issues of old books serve to remind us that black culture and our perceptions of it are always changing. When both *The Norton Anthology of African-American Literature* and *The Oxford Companion to African-American Literature* were published in 1997, for example, they immeasurably altered the status of the world out of which Morrison writes, yet six of her nine novels appeared before they did. To recognize fully the invested nature of her relationship with black culture, we need to remember that "Toni Morrison" was not always a household name, and that black literature was not always in vogue.

Slavery, the American Civil War, and Reconstruction

The sine qua non of African-American experience is – obviously enough – slavery. The first African slaves were taken to what is now the United States by the Spanish in 1526; in 1619 twenty Africans were taken to Jamestown, Virginia, on a Dutch ship and were sold as indentured servants; and 1623 saw the birth of the first black child in the English North American colonies.[1] In her ninth novel, *A Mercy*, through the characters of Florens, Sorrow, and the never-enslaved African blacksmith, Morrison explores the fluid and ambiguous status of people of African descent in late seventeenth-century New England. The Separatist community's dumbfounded response to Florens likewise constitutes a response to blackness before it became automatically associated with slave status, before rigid hierarchies on racial grounds became codified in the two centuries that followed.

While none of Morrison's novels directly treats the late eighteenth century – *Paradise* does so implicitly – the paradoxes of the Enlightenment reverberate in all her novels. One remarkable late eighteenth-century figure is Phillis Wheatley, a Boston-based slave woman who was freed after the publication of her *Poems on Various Subjects, Religious and Moral* in 1773. The way Wheatley's ostensibly conventional neoclassical poems subvert Graeco-Roman tradition to further her emancipatory agenda may well have influenced Morrison's own subversive classical allusiveness. But a more obvious influence on the contemporary writer are the slave narratives, published between 1789 and the 1860s. Written by Olaudah Equiano, Frederick Douglass, William Wells Brown (whose 1853 novel *Clotel* is also important), Harriet Jacobs, and others, these texts sold well during the antebellum years of abolitionist activity but were then not widely available until the late twentieth century. As Morrison writes in "The Site of Memory," "no slave society wrote more – or more thoughtfully – about its own enslavement" (*WMM* 69). She has described "the matrix of the work" that she does as a development of their perspectives, as an articulation of slaves' "interior life" (*WMM* 70).

The authors of the slave narratives, Morrison writes, "knew that literacy was power" because it was illegal for slaves to read and write (*WMM* 68); it is highly significant that Florens, in *A Mercy*, can do both. Morrison is equally interested in the unwritten (but equally subversive) traditions of nineteenth-century black America, however: in the religious forms of the spiritual and the sermon; in vernacular forms of expression such as work chants, storytelling, and quilt making; and in African-American folklores and customs that are a blend of African and American myths and beliefs. Black oral traditions are a vital component of *Beloved*, in which a lullaby and Sethe's story about the earrings are the means by which she recognizes the ghost for who she is, and in which Baby Suggs's preaching in the Clearing is so memorable. Morrison grew up immersed in these traditions and in the more modern musical and rhetorical forms they evolved into, but for those less well versed than she, there are wonderful selections of music and oratory in the *Norton Anthology*, which includes an audio CD.

The American Civil War of 1861–5 figures largely in the life of *Beloved*'s roaming Paul D, but Morrison devotes more narrative space to the postwar era known as Reconstruction and to its aftermath: to the suffering and dislocation its many failures and unfulfilled promises entailed for African-Americans in the South. This is also the subject of *The Souls of Black Folk*, published in 1903 by W. E. B. Du Bois, whose work is a key influence on the contemporary author. It is after the passing of laws enforcing segregation in the late 1870s, which were known as "Jim Crow" and lasted in various forms until the 1950s, that in *Jazz* Rose Dear and her family are dispossessed and whites burn the town of Vienna, and that in *Paradise* the "8-rock" families migrate to Oklahoma from Louisiana and Mississippi. The experience of these families epitomizes the uprootedness or homelessness that is a recurring theme in African-American experience. The forced removal of ancestral Africans from their homelands of course reverberates here, and it is highly significant that the utopian vision at the end of *Paradise* includes "the unambivalent bliss of going home to be at home" (*P* 318).

Black Migration and Urbanization

The dates of what has come to be known as the "Great Migration" – the mass movement of black people from the rural South to the urban North – are contested, but most relocation occurred between 1910 and 1940. It is estimated that by 1920 around 500,000 African-Americans had already left behind the violence and insecurity of the South for the North's promise of better paid jobs in its burgeoning industries and of greater racial tolerance. These decades were the heyday of jazz and the blues, both of which were African-American in origin. Of course, Morrison's *Jazz* – in which Joe and Violet "dance" throughout the train ride that takes them from Virginia to "the City" – is the novel most obviously concerned with the black exodus to the urban Promised Land (*J* 32), but the Great Migration is also an important context in *The Bluest Eye*, in which Cholly and Pauline have come to Lorain from Kentucky, and in *Song of Solomon*, in which Macon Dead I (Jake) and Sing move north to Pennsylvania. These novels dramatize the exhilaration at newfound freedoms combined with the disillusionment at persisting racial discrimination, violence, and economic disenfranchisement that many African-Americans encountered in the North. Black ambivalence about urban life is reflected in what Ralph Ellison has often described as the "tragi-comic" mood of jazz and the blues.

There were several contrasting – and often conflicting – approaches to and movements for black progress in the early twentieth century. Marcus Garvey's United Negro Improvement Association, founded in 1914, promoted the notion of a triumphant return to Africa by displaced people of African descent. Booker T. Washington, who founded the Tuskegee Institute in Alabama in 1881, prioritized vocational training and manual labor for blacks over intellectual education and suffrage. Du Bois, who was explicitly critical of Washington's accommodationist stance, founded (along with many others) the NAACP (National Association for the Advancement of Colored People) in 1909. The contrasting perspectives of these leaders informed the divisions within the later civil rights movement, and in *Song of Solomon, Jazz, Paradise*, and *Love* Morrison's characters articulate the unresolved differences between the by-now-mythologized figureheads.

The NAACP's monthly magazine, *The Crisis*, quickly replaced Pauline Hopkins's *Colored American Magazine* as the primary vehicle of black political and artistic expression. A forum for key authors such as Charles Chesnutt and James Weldon Johnson, and of the defining writers of the Harlem Renaissance such as Jessie Fauset, Langston Hughes, Countee Cullen, and Jean Toomer, it created and reflected a cultural vibrancy (matched by innovation in the musical and visual arts) that finds expression in *Jazz*. Morrison's take on the Harlem of the 1920s is not uncritical: in skeptical dialogue with Alain Locke and the thesis of his 1925 anthology *The New Negro*, she has questioned the white investment in black culture and the promotion of primitive art that, as the novels of Nella Larsen show, were a feature of this time.

Morrison's representations of the first half of the twentieth century pay as much attention to black participation in the two world wars, to race riots, and to the persistence of black poverty during the depression of the 1930s and 1940s as they do to cultural innovation and celebration. Zora Neale Hurston's spirited writing is an influential document of black rural life at this time, and although Morrison did not read her until she had completed *Song of Solomon* (*DC* 102), she is a significant crucial "ancestor" to the contemporary writer. In eschewing the distinction between aesthetics and politics, Morrison implicitly eschews the conventional juxtaposition between the "experimental" writing epitomized by Hurston and the "protest novel" exemplified by Richard Wright's *Native Son* (1940). *The Bluest Eye, Sula*, and *Song of Solomon*, for example, clearly confront the political realities of the 1930s and 1940s but do so in artistically innovative form. They also give close attention to key cultural institutions such as the black church, an organization Morrison has labeled "the most pragmatic and realistic institution we ever had" (*WMM* 35).

From the 1950s and 1960s to the Present Day

The murder of Emmett Till in 1955 (the focus of *Dreaming Emmett* and a key referent in *Song of Solomon*) is often viewed as one of the catalysts or defining beginnings of the civil rights movement. Landmark moments of this era, such as the student sit-ins of 1960 or the bomb that killed four schoolgirls in a church in Birmingham, Alabama, in 1963, punctuate *Solomon* and *Paradise*. As well as the successes of the movement, its divisions, for example, over the use of retaliatory violence, and the problematic aspects of its leadership and rhetoric are dramatized through the actions of Guitar in *Song of Solomon*, and through the experiences of Reverend Misner in *Paradise* and of Christine in *Love*. *Song of Solomon* is also the work most obviously in dialogue with Ellison's *Invisible Man* and indebted to James Baldwin's explorations of black masculinity. The two later novels also examine other central upheavals of the American 1960s: the war in Vietnam, the sexual revolution, and the assassinations of key political heroes such as Malcolm X (in 1965) and Martin Luther King and Robert Kennedy (both in 1968).

It is no coincidence that Morrison sets *Paradise*, with its focus on a handful of dispossessed girls, in the decade in which second wave feminism was at its zenith: the 1970s. Such ironic counterpointing is typical of Morrison's refusal to accept mythologized history at its face value. This was also the decade characterized by dynamism of the Black Arts movement, however, led by the poet and playwright Amiri Baraka, and it heralded a flowering of literary production by African-American women including Toni Cade Bambara (edited by Morrison), Alice Walker, and of course Morrison herself. At the same time, black women critics were rediscovering and republishing the long-obscured work of their literary ancestors such as Hurston and Larsen.

From this time on, Morrison both as author and as editor was making and remaking the African-American scene; she was influencing it as much as it was influencing her. In 1993, she described her first novel as a series of "attempts to transfigure the complexity and wealth of Black-American culture into a language worthy of the culture" (*BE*172). It is clear that this is exactly what her work has done. Yet in the same piece, she writes that her "narrative project is as difficult today as it was thirty years ago." Has it become any easier now? The publication of *A Mercy* coincided almost exactly with the election of Barack Obama to the presidency of the United States. As this book goes to press, his reelection to a second term hangs in the balance. Change has certainly come to America, but the precise nature and the full extent of that change remain to be seen.

Morrison and Dominant American Culture

In *Playing in the Dark*, Morrison observes that "for the most part, the literature of the United States has taken as its concern the architecture of a new white man" (*PiD* 14–15). In the same chapter, she defines "the major and championed characteristics" of the "national literature" as "individualism; masculinity, social engagement versus historical isolation; acute and ambiguous moral problematics" (5). She writes, with reference to "that well-fondled phrase, 'the American Dream,'" that "the desire for freedom is preceded by oppression; a yearning for God's law is born of the detestation of human license and corruption" and "the glamor of riches is in thrall to poverty, hunger, and debt" (*PiD* 33, 35). While her purpose in *Playing in the Dark* is literary criticism, and her aim to explore how a fabricated "Africanism" functions within canonical Euro-American texts, her own fiction consistently engages in dialogue with the ideologies expressed not just by those texts but by the whole national culture of which they form one part. Major impulses in the Morrisonian oeuvre are the dismantling of national narratives, a challenge to the flaws inherent in the myths of national self-definition, and a re-envisioning of what "Americanness" might mean.

As I have already discussed, each of Morrison's novels operates within several timeframes simultaneously. The allegorical nature of much of her writing enables her to allude to key moments in America's past, often connecting them to events set in recent times. Both *A Mercy* and *Tar Baby*, for example, function on one level as allegories about the "discovery" and European conquest of America from the end of the fifteenth century onward. Through Valerian's marriage to the child-bride Margaret and through Cosey's to the eleven-year-old Heed, the author parodies the configuration of America as a virgin land, despoiled by an all-conquering hero that has been, from the canonical discovery narratives to *The Great Gatsby*, something of a refrain in the national literature. She is also able to comment on the present through events set in the past. In *A Mercy*, for example, she illuminates the post-9/11 "axis of evil" mind-set while exploring the late 1600s.

Through her trademark allusiveness, Morrison constructs a revisionary conversation with the key texts that combine to form mainstream accounts of U.S. history. Valerie Babb has demonstrated the extent to which *A Mercy*, in its alternative portrait of late seventeenth-century New England, Maryland, and Virginia, engages and "re-places" the myth of origins that was formed by early texts about those colonies by William Bradford, John Winthrop, and John Smith.[2] As my discussions in Chapter 2 make clear, both *A Mercy* and *Paradise* critique the Puritan worldview, and in particular the attempt to fix binary oppositions. They expose the dominant American preoccupation with the threat of an external but containable evil that is expressed in works such as Cotton Mather's *Magnalia Christi Americana* (1702) and explored in the writings of Nathaniel Hawthorne.

The America of the late eighteenth and early nineteenth centuries – of the Founding Fathers and the foundation of the new republic from the revolution beginning in 1776 – is also, of course, a central concern in *Paradise*. The patriarchs of Ruby create a flawed, exclusivist utopian settlement, as did Thomas Jefferson and the revolutionary heroes after whom many of the characters in that novel are named. The fact that some characters in *Paradise* are also given classical names mocks the Founding Fathers' widespread veneration of the classical world and their belief in their project's analogical relationship to both the Athenian democracy and the Roman Republic. In this novel as well as in *Love*, Morrison subjects to scrutiny the Euro-American tradition of the individual hero, whose actions are made to define national ideals, and of the isolated single protagonist celebrated in works such as R. W. B. Lewis's study *The American Adam* (1955) and other key texts in the 1950s American studies/liberal tradition. Together with the novelist's oeuvrewide concern with the relationship between communities and individuals, this process of motivated intertextuality contributes to the challenge to individualism that the novels constitute.

Morrison's interest in the culture of the late 1700s/early 1800s includes her skeptical perspective on many of the central tenets of Enlightenment thought. While the familiar irony that the Declaration of Independence fails to abolish slavery is key, in her seminal essay "The Site of Memory" the author reminds us that the "Age of Enlightenment" had a "twin, born at the same time, the Age of Scientific Racism" (*WMM* 69). The racial theories of Hume, Kant, Jefferson, and others, derived from innovations in classificatory systems by scientists such as Linnaeus, have been collected in useful readers such as Emmanuel Chukwudi Eze's anthology *Race and the Enlightenment* (1997). The well-read, race-obsessed Soaphead Church in *The Bluest Eye* is the inevitable product of these theories, while schoolteacher and his notebook in *Beloved* are agent and instrument of that same oppressive "age." Many items included in *The Black Book* evidence a persistent pseudoscientific interest in black people, and Morrison's oeuvre is replete with characters who like to categorize and demarcate: Pauline in *The Bluest Eye*, Nel in *Sula*, Jadine in *Tar Baby*, and the Founding Fathers in *Paradise* have all absorbed and exhibit a tendency toward classification passed down to them from Enlightenment thought. The racism of more recent dominant culture, as well, including the insidious effects of the racialized systems defining conceptions of value and physical beauty that Hollywood culture perpetuates, is a central theme in the novels set in recent times, and the author illuminates modern racism's debt to Enlightenment structures in these texts.

It is important to recognize the extent to which Morrison engages and takes issue with Euro-American narratives about slavery, the Civil War, and the American South. *Beloved*, for example, works against the representation of the fall of the Old South and the doomed Confederate cause as tragedy, which is epitomized by films such as *The Birth of a Nation* (1915) and *Gone with the Wind* (1939) and by some impulses in the novels of William Faulkner. In *Jazz*, meanwhile, the author takes to task both the pastoralism on which constructions of the Old South depend (in texts ranging from the writings of Thomas Jefferson to the collection by the "Southern Agrarianists" *I'll Take My Stand*, published in 1930) and the depiction of miscegenation as catastrophic that is another feature of white writing about the South such as Faulkner's. Morrison's engagement with Mark Twain, meanwhile, is more like her relationship to Melville; she is interested in putting pressure on the fault lines in his own position, in exploring the vistas toward which he gestures but cannot fully articulate.

As I have discussed in Chapter 2, in *Jazz* Morrison voices an alternative version of the "Jazz Age," of modern American urban life, to that reified by *The Great Gatsby*. Her interest in the relationship between slavery and the dislocations that characterize modernity also places her work, and that same novel in particular, in dialogue with canonical modernists such as T. S. Eliot and with white women writers such as Willa Cather, who have enjoyed the privileges of their whiteness but have been subject to the setbacks of their gender. Morrison's ambivalent engagement with the feminist movement(s) of the American 1950s–1970s finds expression in *Paradise* and *Love* as well as in her early polemic, "What the Black Woman Things about Woman's Lib" (1971). Alongside her negotiations of the civil rights movement in these novels is her treatment of other momentous aspects of the American 1950s, the decade in which *Home*, too, is primarily set, and the 1960s. These include McCarthyism (which also resonates in *A Mercy*), the assassinations of the Kennedy brothers, and the Korean and Vietnam Wars. The primary setting of *Love* is Morrison's most contemporary to date, and (like *Sula*) it concerns itself with what has been lost as well gained in the transition from a racially segregated to a (purportedly) racially integrated nation.

Morrison and African Cultures and Traditions

After reading from *A Mercy* at the Toni Morrison Society Conference in Charleston, South Carolina (July 2008), Morrison was asked by a member of the audience whether she had ever visited Africa or had any plans to visit. She answered that she had never been there, that recent health issues had prevented her from making a planned trip to South Africa, and that she now had no plans to go. "How could I? How could I go to Africa now, at my age?" she asked in reply. What she gestures toward but does not articulate here speaks volumes about the significance of that continent in her consciousness and in her work.

Morrison did not encounter any African literature until after she had completed her formal education at Cornell (in 1955). Her work as editor, novelist, and public commentator in subsequent decades, however, has frequently testified to her interest in and familiarity with both North African (particularly Egyptian and Ethiopian) and West African cultures and traditions. As I discuss at more length in Chapter 4, scholars such as La Vinia Delois Jennings (in *Toni Morrison and the Idea of Africa*, 2008) have painstakingly illuminated the engagement in Morrison's fiction with the belief systems and cosmologies of Dahomey, Kongo, and Yoruba people, while my own work has documented her allusiveness to ancient Egyptian and Ethiopian cultures. In my essay on "the Africanness of classicism" in her work, I argue that through allusions in *Sula, Tar Baby, Jazz,* and *Paradise* she enters into dialogue with Afrocentric arguments about Egypt and/or Nubia as the "origin" of Western civilization.[3]

In *Tar Baby*, for example, the tree spirits are "arrogant ... knowing as they did that the first world of the world had been built with their sacred properties; that they alone could hold together the stone of pyramids and the rushes of Moses's crib" (*TB* 183), while in *Paradise* Richard Misner fantasizes about an African "real earthly home" that precedes Western civilization (*P* 213). In such passages, Morrison participates in a tradition (peopled by, among others, Frederick Douglass, W. E. B. Du Bois, Pauline Hopkins, and Ishmael Reed) that is known in some quarters as "Ethiopianism" – a strategic African-American identification with the power and cultural richness of this region of Northeast Africa in order to further the black American emancipatory agenda. Since the beginnings of the abolition movement, activists and literary writers have drawn inspiration from the prophecy of Psalm 68 ('Princes shall come out of Egypt and Ethiopia') and have consciously fabricated or performed a connection between these ancient civilizations and Americans of African descent in order to advance their cause. In its nod to the ancient Egyptian Book of the Dead, the book of photographs by James Van der Zee and text entitled *The Harlem Book of the Dead* (to which Morrison wrote the foreword in 1978) exemplifies the significance of ancient Egypt in African-American culture.

In Chapter 2, I discuss Morrison's epigraphs to *Jazz* and *Paradise*, which are taken from the Gnostic Gospel texts dating from the third and fourth centuries CE and collected in the Nag Hammadi library. These texts are written in Coptic, the Egyptian language written in the Greek alphabet, and so testify to the historical relationships of ancient Egypt, ancient Greece, and Christianity, and to the cultural syncretism to which first Greek and then Roman conquests of Egypt gave rise. This relationship and this syncretism hold great appeal for Morrison. Indeed, her engagement with the Nag Hammadi texts is just one example of her interest in African and classical intersections, an interest that may explain the presences of *both* those inheritances in her work. For besides her concern with the connections between ancient Egypt, Greece, and Rome, she has spoken frequently of her sense of an affinity between West African and Greek culture and tradition. In a 1985 interview Morrison describes Greek tragedy as "extremely sympathetic to Black culture and in some ways to African culture" (*TG* 181), while in "Unspeakable Things Unspoken" she writes that she feels "intellectually at home" in Greek tragedy because of "its similarity to Afro-American communal structures … and African religion and philosophy" (*UTU* 2). To illuminate these points is of course not to suggest that Morrison is only interested in West African traditions because of her interest in the classics; it is rather to suggest how she maintains and engages with two bodies of culture that might on first glance appear politically incompatible. Her excitement about West African literature and her familiarity with West African traditions in their own right are tangible and widespread, as I go on to discuss.

In the 1970s, while an editor at Random House, Morrison published two anthologies that provide ample evidence of her wish to promote African literature in the United States. The first, *Contemporary African Literature* (edited by Edris Makward and Leslie Lacy, listing Morrison as the "project editor"), appeared in 1972. It includes tales and legends, short stories, novel excerpts, poetry, excerpted drama, and nonfictional essays by forty-three authors hailing from West, Southern, and East Africa, of whom the most well known today include the Nigerian novelist Chinua Achebe, the Ghanaian novelist Ama Ata Aidoo, the South African playwright Athol Fugard, the South African novelist Bessie Head, the Guinean novelist Camara Laye, the Kenyan theologian John S. Mbiti, the Senegalese poet Leopold Senghor, the Nigerian playwright Wole Soyinka, and the Kenyan author Ngugi Wa Thiong'o (then known as James Ngugi). The second anthology, *Giant Talk: An Anthology of Third World Writings*, edited by Quincy Troupe and Rainer Schulte, appeared in 1975; it includes writing by Achebe, Aidoo, Senghor, Soyinka, Thiong'o, and the Nigerian novelist Amos Tutuola, alongside a wide range of African-American, Latin American, Native American, and other non-European/non-Euro-American authors. To know that Morrison was acquainted with such a broad range of African writing in the early years of her own novelistic career is central to an understanding of her work, and to what, as Jennings has emphasized, she has labeled the "elusive but identifiable" blackness that characterizes it (*WMM* 61).

Morrison has frequently expressed her enthusiasm for specific African texts in interviews. For example, in 1986, she describes her reading of Camara Laye's *The Radiance of the King* (published in 1954, originally written in French and titled *Le Regard du Roi*) as "a very narcotic kind of experience, a journey for me that was overwhelming, quite" (*TG* 228). In 2001, Morrison published a long review of the novel in the *New York Review of Books*, in which she describes her encounter with it as "shocking." This essay (*WMM* 118–32) repays careful reading as an authorial meditation on her changing perceptions of the nature of Africa and African literature as a whole. She highlights the way this novelist "reinvents" the "clichéd journey to African darkness," using "the idiom of the conqueror" to "pluck at the Western eye" and preparing it "to meet the 'regard,' the 'look,' the 'gaze' of an African King" (*WMM* 121–2). Her comparison of this author to "a blacksmith, transforming a red-hot lump of iron into a worthy blade" sits interestingly beside *A Mercy* (*WMM* 122), while the early pages of this essay constitute a significant appraisal of the trajectories that twentieth-century African literature followed. She has also expressed her admiration, in interviews, for Achebe ("a *real* education"), for Soyinka, for Ayi Kwei Armah ("books that one can re-read with enormous discoveries subsequently"), and for Bessie Head (*TG* 228–30). In 1994 she commended Achebe, Laye, Head, and Senghor for the fact that they "did not explain their black world." They "took their blackness as central and the whites were the 'other'" (*DC* 102).

Besides Morrison's clear positioning of black people at the center of her fiction, and her refusal to write for and/or clarify her literary worlds for white readers, Morrison's debt to West African traditions manifests itself most clearly in her interest in the survivals or retentions of African cultures in African-American culture. Her acknowledgment of West African influences on the African-American worldview – such as in the community's conception of evil and urge to scapegoat in *Sula*, or in Pilate's ways of knowing and special powers in *Song of Solomon*, or in the nature of Baby Suggs's spirituality or Beloved's desire for vengeance in *Beloved* – is key to the challenge to the rationality of Enlightenment-bred dominant American culture that I have explored earlier in this chapter. As Jennings has demonstrated, the resonances of West African religious beliefs and practices – including the centrality of Kongo's *Yowa* (cosmogram, a cross or tree within a circle), and concepts of "witches," "living elders," and "specialists" or priest/healer figures – are ubiquitous in Morrison's work. Likewise the presences of Voudoun, Voodoo, and Candomblé traditions – that is to say, of the black diasporic practices to which transatlantic slavery gave rise and that are derived from West African spiritual systems – are an important feature of Morrison's landscapes. Ultimately, to recognize the full significance of Africa in Morrison's work is to recognize the extent to which she gives voice not just to black America but to a transnational black experience, and in doing so shapes our perceptions not just of the United States but of the modern world as a whole.

Morrison, Transnational Perspectives, Modernism, and Postmodernism

Although the nature of U.S. history and identity is one of Morrison's primary concerns, not one of her novels is without reference either to non-U.S. locations and identities or to events that involve America but do not take place on its soil. In *The Bluest Eye*, for example, Soaphead Church is of mixed English and African descent, an immigrant from the Caribbean. At the start of *Sula*, Shadrack has just returned from fighting in World War I in France (and this war makes its presence felt in *Jazz* as well), while *Song of Solomon* opens with Robert Smith's ill-fated ambition to fly to Canada and details a smell (as Milkman and Guitar are about to rob Pilate) that recalls "a marketplace in Accra" (*SoS* 184). *Beloved* stages a version of the Middle Passage from West Africa; *Paradise* encompasses the American military deployment in the Pacific region during World War II, as well as the Vietnam War and Consolata's early life in Brazil; in *Love* Christine spends her brief and unhappy marriage to Ernie Holder in Germany, where he is stationed (post World War II) with other American troops; and *Home* centers on the experiences of a veteran of the Korean War. Morrison's consistent depiction of the United States as one country that exists in relation to many others works against American exceptionalism. To some extent her fiction anticipates, or at the very least corresponds with, theoretical moves toward a transnational positioning of America that work against nationalistic privileging of that country as a self-contained, unique, and superior entity.

The novels that are most explicitly transnational in outlook are of course *Tar Baby* and *A Mercy*. The former involves Jadine's years in Paris and the Caribbean setting of Isle des Chevaliers, where Gideon and Thérèse are among the non-U.S. black population. The latter demonstrates that in the late seventeenth-century globalization of a sort was already a reality: Morrison explores the inextricable links that the economic imperatives of slavery and colonialism between Europe – specifically Portugal and London – Africa (specifically Angola), the Caribbean (specifically Barbados), and the American colonies of Virginia, Maryland, and New England. *Tar Baby* anticipates and *A Mercy* exemplifies Paul Gilroy's paradigm-shifting theory of "the black

Atlantic," which he published in the book of the same name, *The Black Atlantic: Modernity and Double-Consciousness*, in 1993. Gilroy defines the black Atlantic as a "transcultural, international formation," one that is best illustrated by "the image of ships in motion across the spaces between Europe, America, Africa and the Caribbean."[4] Gilroy also exposes the fact that black nationalist thought has had to "repress its own ambivalence about exile from Africa" (ix); Morrison's novels are profoundly concerned with this ambivalence: the fact, for example, that Joe Trace trips over "black roots" while looking for his mother in *Jazz* resonates with Paul Gilroy's assertion that a focus on "routes" rather than "roots" and "rootedness" is a productive model for political change (*J* 179; Gilroy 19).

Gilroy devotes a few pages of his book to a discussion of *Beloved* and of the Margaret Garner case (64–9; 217–22), and his theory of "the black Atlantic" has functioned as the sine qua non of transnational scholarship on the novelist such as Alan Rice's in *Radical Narratives of the Black Atlantic* (2003) or my own in the *African Athena* volume (2011). And as I discuss in Chapter 4, Morrison's work is also cast in a different but connected transnational perspective by her significance within the field of postcolonial studies, for example, in the work of Homi Bhabha or Jonathan White. Related to Morrison's engagement with a global black diasporic experience, and with the United States as one player on a global stage, is the still-evolving transnational nature of the reception of her work. Translated into numerous languages, studied in universities from South Africa to Japan, Morrison is now an author of global stature and significance. The Toni Morrison Society Conference in Paris in November 2010 marked something of a watershed moment – the first event of its kind to be held outside the United States, it included scholars from every continent, whose readings of her work took for granted and worked within her status as a central figure in transnational intellectual history.

One of Morrison's most significant contributions to the analysis of global culture is to recent understanding of the nature of modernity, modernism, and postmodernism, and of the relationship between these processes. Her transnational outlook is fundamental to her challenge to Eurocentric conceptualizations of modernity and its cultural forms, as her 1988 interview with Paul Gilroy, "Living Memory," and her 1998 interview with Carolyn Denard make clear. Morrison sees the dislocations produced by the enforced migration of African peoples as the catalyst to the modern condition: "Modern life begins with slavery," she says. "Black women had to deal with 'post-modern' problems in the nineteenth century and earlier. These things had to be addressed by black people a long time ago. Certain kinds of dissolution, the loss of and the need to reconstruct certain kinds of stability."[5] It is arguable that Morrison's words here influenced Gilroy's formulation, published five years later, of the black Atlantic as a "counterculture of modernity" (Gilroy 1). The novelist develops her thinking on this subject in her discussion with Denard, where she asserts that "the [American] South is where the black experiment begins." She explains that "what people did in this country was brand new. Even if they did it a long time ago. These people were very inventive, very creative and that was a very modern situation" (*DC* 193). As *Jazz* makes manifest, Morrison's concern is less to create or contribute to the idea of a "black modernism" distinct from (an implicitly white) "modernism" but rather to alter the nature of what is meant by the unqualified term "modernism" itself.

One critic profoundly concerned with the question of Morrison's relationship to modernism and postmodernism is John Duvall, whose book *The Identifying Fictions of Toni Morrison* (2000) is subtitled *Modernist Authenticity and Postmodern Blackness*. Although the novelist does not advocate the conceptualization of an essential black modernism, Duvall argues that in her early novels Morrison does argue for an essentialist "distinctive black difference" and does so "in a particularly modernist fashion," because she maintains that "African-American authenticity ... exceeds the medium of language."[6] The critic goes on to suggest that "if Morrison's content recalls modernist concern with authenticity, her techniques, particularly in her more recent novels, suggest certain postmodern fictional practices." Duvall argues that Morrison's postmodernism is not the kind exemplified by "a set of highly aestheticized novels that produced very limited political engagement," but rather the more politically engaged definition of postmodernism formulated by Linda Hutcheon, that of "historiographical metafiction." In Hutcheon's definition, "all attempts to construe the past are interpretive," and this kind of fiction is inherently antihierarchical.[7]

This complex area of discussion about Morrison is not completely resolved even by Duvall's careful and persuasive arguments, however. While Morrison indisputably deploys the techniques of literary postmodernism in novels such as *Beloved*, *Jazz*, and *Paradise*, one wonders what she would make of the relativism implicit in the idea that "all attempts to construe the past are interpretive." Were transatlantic slavery and the multiple abuses it entailed an absolute reality? They were – and to bring the nature of their reality and their legacy into sharper and more complete focus is surely at the heart of Morrison's project. As this necessarily brief discussion of broad and complex issues has made clear, the exact nature of Morrison's position in relation to transnational modernism and postmodernism is neither fixed nor easily resolved. What is indisputable, however, is that her role within these formations is a major one.

Chapter 4

Reception

The Critical Field

In an introductory book of this kind, it is neither possible nor helpful to attempt a comprehensive overview of the copious and always-growing scholarship on Morrison's work. What follows is a broad account of key lines of inquiry and of dispute in the critical field, arranged by decade from the 1970s to the present day. The "story" of Morrison criticism has not, of course, followed a logical, systematic progression, and nor is it characterized by the predominance of any one approach over another. It is always related to broader developments in the fields of race, gender, comparative literary studies, and many others, and for this reason this section of the book is best read not in isolation but together with Chapter 3, "Contexts," and with the account of Morrison's criticism of her own work (and that of others) in Chapter 2. In the "Guide to Further Reading" I have listed (with full bibliographical information) all the essay collections, journal articles, and monographs quoted in this section, together with general recommendations. Page references for quotations from the works listed there are cited parenthetically in this text.

The 1970s

In the introduction to *Toni Morrison: Critical and Theoretical Approaches* (1997), Nancy Peterson gives a useful account of the earliest scholarly responses to Morrison. The first academic article on Morrison was published in the fall of 1975 in a now-defunct journal, *Studies in Black Literature*; it is Joan Bischcoff's "The Novels of Toni Morrison: Studies in Thwarted Sensitivity" (Peterson, *Toni* 3). This article, like several of the earliest mainstream reviews of *The Bluest Eye* and *Sula* reprinted in the Gates and Appiah collection, *Toni Morrison Critical Perspectives Past and Present* (1993), struggles to reconcile Morrison's specific focus on African-American experience with her universalism. A white Euro-American subject position is assumed in these early responses, to which Morrison's concerns are always cast as relative. Sarah Blackburn writes in the

New York Times of *Sula*, for example, that "one continually feels its narrowness, its refusal to brim over into the world outside its provincial setting," and that the author is "far too talented to remain only a marvelous recorder of the black side of provincial American life" (Gates and Appiah 8).

As Peterson records, the first critical analyses of Morrison by black scholars appeared in the now-difficult-to-locate glossy magazine *First World* (winter 1977); here Philip Royster addresses *The Bluest Eye* and Odette C. Martin writes on *Sula*. Their placing the author alongside Du Bois, Hurston, and others insists that Morrison be viewed first and foremost as an African-American author, who emerged from and herself extended a broader African-American tradition that was being documented and given scholarly validation at exactly this time. Writing in 2012, when there is now an equally significant move to free African-American culture from categorical confines, it is easy to lose sight of the radicalism and necessity of this kind of definition, and of the struggle it involved. Morrison's own role in that process is evident in her 1976 interview with Robert Stepto, in which she encourages specific new directions in criticism such as analysis of how contemporary black women writers treat "the stereotype of the black woman" (*TG* 26), or a focus on the black female adventurer, or on the black parent as "culture bearer" (*TG* 27). Although Chikwenye Ogunyemi, Phyllis Klotman, and a handful of others published brief pieces on the first two novels in this decade, there were only a few more full-length journal articles at this time: one on "the inverted world" of *The Bluest Eye* and *Sula* by Jacqueline de Weever and the other a lesbian reading of *Sula* by Barbara Smith.[1] In 1980, Barbara Christian included an extensive chapter on these novels in the first book to include critical analysis of Morrison, which was her groundbreaking study *Black Women Novelists: The Development of a Tradition 1892–1976*. The fact that she referred to none of the 1970s scholarship on Morrison whatsoever is indicative of the insubstantiality of the field in those early years.

1980s

The critical attention paid to Morrison became slowly but steadily more extensive in the early 1980s; that increase was due partly to the emergence of black feminist discourse and partly to the fanfare that greeted *Song of Solomon* in 1977. In a book that implicitly answers Morrison's suggestions to Robert Stepto, in that it aims "to trace the development of stereotypical images imposed on black women," Barbara Christian's substantial chapter "The Contemporary Fables of Toni Morrison" raises many of the key issues that later critics go on to develop (Christian x). The critic describes Morrison's first two novels as "fantastic earthy realism," "rooted in history and mythology," and observes that their themes develop "in much the same way as a good jazz musician finds the hidden melodies within a musical phrase" (Christian 137). She illuminates the extent to which the community acts as "hindrances" in both novels and is keenly attuned to the aural qualities of the writing, to what she calls "our society's sound" (Christian 152).

Among the flurry of scholarly articles on *Song of Solomon* that appeared during the early 1980s, one of the most significant is Cynthia Davis's study "Self, Society and Myth."[2] This is a discussion of all the novels from *The Bluest Eye* to *Tar Baby* that perceptively distinguishes Morrison's project from Ellison's, highlighting the ways that Morrison eschews black invisibility. Susan Willis's well-known essay "Eruptions of Funk: Historicizing Toni Morrison" also appeared in this year and also addresses all of the first four novels.[3] Willis (who includes comparison with Faulkner) argues that "sexuality converges with history and functions as a register for the experience of change, i.e. historical transition" (Gates and Appiah 308). Defining "funk" as the "intrusion" of a "not-so-distant social mode" into "the present" (Gates and Appiah 325), she examines, from a materialist perspective, each novel's subversive engagement with the specific era in which it is set. In her much-anthologized 1983 article "A Hateful Passion, a Lost Love," meanwhile, Hortense Spillers illuminates the radicalism of *Sula* and of Sula, distinguishing that eponymous character from Vyry Ware in Margaret Walker's *Jubilee* (1966) and Janie in Hurston's *Their Eyes Were Watching God*.[4] Morrison continued to feature in overview studies of African-American writing at this time, as well. Mari Evans's edited anthology *Black Women Writers: 1950–80* (1984), for example, includes two essays about Morrison as well as publishing Morrison's own essay, "Rootedness," while Keith Byerman's monograph *Fingering the Jagged Grain* (1985) includes a chapter comparing Morrison with Gayl Jones.

In a 1983 interview with Nellie McKay, Morrison articulates her sense that critics must bring an understanding of cultural specificity to her work; her words have been much discussed ever since. In asking for "pioneering work to be done in literary criticism," she insists, "I am not *like* James Joyce; I am not *like* Thomas Hardy; I am not *like* Faulkner. I am not *like* in that sense" (*TG* 152). The question of Morrison in comparative context, of the authors to whom she might be compared without a diminishing of her own project, has never gone away but rather has grown in complexity and nuance over the decades. Morrison's point in these words is surely that her aesthetic innovativeness and her specific politics be given their due; that something be done to intervene in the discourse of critics who, as she puts it earlier in the same interview, "don't evolve out of the culture, the world, the given quality out of which I write," and in Eurocentric processes by which "other kinds of structures are imposed on [her] works" (*TG* 151). While this caveat is well taken, and much work on Morrison's relationship to African-American and African cultures has followed, many scholars have consistently refused to avoid drawing comparisons between Morrison and European and Euro-American authors.

Indeed, the very first book to devote itself entirely to Toni Morrison – *The World of Toni Morrison: Explorations in Literary Criticism* by Bessie Jones and Audrey Vinson (1985) – locates her in its first chapter within "the grotesque as an American genre in the tradition of writers which include Sherwood Anderson, ... Flannery O'Connor, Eudora Welty and William Faulkner" (16). In 2012 such a move would provoke less anxiety than it might in the nascent identity-politics-structured culture of 1985. This same culture is reflected in the title of the second book to appear on Morrison, *New Dimensions of Spirituality: A Biracial and Bicultural Reading of the Novels of Toni Morrison*, by Karla Holloway and Stephanie Demetrakapoulos (1987). It is interesting that the authors felt compelled to identify their own racial identities and the "bicultural" nature of their critical approach. These two critics are in some ways ahead of their time in their awareness of how "Morrison's novels draw us deeper into the relationships of a global culture" (Holloway 4), although their careful negotiations of race and feminism in their introduction indicate their awareness of what is at stake in this claim.

The appearance in 1988 of *Critical Essays on Toni Morrison* (edited by Nellie McKay) was something of a watershed moment; it was the first collection of its kind on this author and is still one of the most useful. It collects reviews with twelve essays, nine of which were written specifically for this volume and most of which (for example, Eleanor Traylor's examination of *Tar Baby*) continue to be key. McKay's introduction argues for an "essence of ancient, authentic blackness" in Morrison's work, based on its affinity with black music (1). Several of her contributors, such as Trudier Harris or Michael Awkward, went on to publish their own monographs about African-American women's writing. Awkward's *Inspiriting Influences: Tradition, Revision, and Afro-American Women's Novels* (1989), for example, is one of several important books that consolidate the concept of, and comprise detailed investigations into, the genealogy of black American writing by women at this time.[5] The first monograph to be published exclusively on Morrison – Terry Otten's slim but significant *The Crime of Innocence* (1989) – adopts an approach that is in many ways the opposite to that of McKay, in that it is not premised on qualities of "blackness" in the writing. Addressing each novel from *The Bluest Eye* to *Beloved* in turn, it identifies the importance of the Bible in Morrison's work and argues that the paradigm of the Fall in Genesis is central in every text: "Each novel describes

a fall wrought with destruction but one that is still morally superior to prolonged self-ignorance and sterile accommodation" (3).

By now – the end of the 1980s – most of the lines of inquiry into Morrison's
work are established, and most of the issues that have continued to divide critics – for example, about the comparative importance of African-American
(and African) or European influences on and concerns within her work,
or to what extent she should be positioned as a "black woman writer" – are
already center stage. Harold Bloom's collection, *Modern Critical Views: Toni
Morrison*, appearing in 1990, republishes many of the most important essays
of the decade that precedes it, as well as "Unspeakable Things Unspoken." That
Morrison by this point should be the subject of a book in this series indicates
the increasing acknowledgment she received from the makers and guarders
of the dominant American canon, yet Bloom is somewhat grudging in his
introduction. Ironically enough, the simultaneously politically engaged and
aesthetically attuned essays he reprints in the collection themselves belie his
impotent wish: "Morrison's five novels ... are possible candidates for entering
an American canon founded upon what I insist would be aesthetic criteria
alone, if we still retain any such criteria after our current age of politicized
response ... has passed" (1). As the next decades in readings of Morrison were
to demonstrate, the politicized horse had well and truly bolted by now.

The 1990s

The year 1990 brought with it a landmark publication in black American
women's literary studies: Joanne Braxton and Andrée McLaughlin's critical
anthology, *Wild Women in the Whirlwind*. The celebratory tone of its editors'
introductory essays could not be more different from the grudging ambivalence of Harold Bloom. Braxton writes of "the literary rebirth of black women
writers during the last twenty years" and of a "wonderful time of opportunity"
(xxi); McLaughlin trumpets "a renaissance of the spirit inspired by those who
have refused to surrender" (Braxton xxxi). A similar newfound confidence
asserts itself in Barbara Hill Rigney's *The Voices of Toni Morrison* (1991), a
much more overtly politicized study than Otten's, which places the novelist's
work within "a black feminine/feminist aesthetic" (1) and claims "a common
ground for theory, race and gender" (5).

Within the *Whirlwind* anthology, Barbara Christian discusses *Beloved* as a
"historical novel" alongside Walker's *The Color Purple* (1982) and Sherley Anne
Williams's *Dessa Rose* (1987), arguing that together these books constitute a
new "trend" and exploring the reasons for their near-simultaneous appearance
in the 1980s (Braxton 326–41). Preceding this, Vashti Crutcher Lewis's essay

"African Tradition in Toni Morrison's *Sula*" argues unequivocally that the novelist writes from an African point of view – an African "aesthetic" – in this novel (Braxton 316–25; 316). She begins by supplying Babangi and "Kongo" translations of the name "Sula" (316). While Kathleen O'Shaugnessy's essay on the African choric elements in *Song of Solomon* (originally published in the McKay 1988 collection) was the first to adopt this approach, it is one that was developed in the 1990s in two essays by Gay Wilentz – one "African Heritage as Cultural Discourse" in the same novel (1992), the other "An African-Based Reading of *Sula*" (1997).[6] Often implicit in these early studies of Morrison's use of West African traditions is the suggestion of these as her primary, most important, and even exclusive cultural resource.

At the same time, there was a growing and at this stage contrapuntal interest in the author's engagement with Graeco-Roman traditions (and, as I go on to discuss, it was not until a decade later that critics theorized the productive coexistence of *both* African and classical presences in the texts). While in the 1980s critics such as Holloway and Demetrakapoulos or Jones and Vinson had discussed the allusions to Ovid and to Greek tragedy in Morrison's novels, in 1991 Kimberly Benston published the most nuanced essay to date on this subject, "Re-weaving the 'Ulysses Scene'."[7] In interpreting Morrison's revisionary perspective on classical paradigms in both literary-aesthetic and psychoanalytic terms, Benston's approach had much in common with that of Marianne Hirsch, whose major publication *The Mother Daughter Plot: Narrative, Psychoanalysis, Feminism* (1989) includes important discussion of *Sula* and *Beloved*. Among the many psychoanalytical readings of Morrison is Jennifer Fitzerald's essay on selfhood and community in *Beloved*, which appeared in the *Modern Fiction Studies* special issue on Morrison of 1993. The appearance of this double issue was a landmark in the field – at once a demonstration of the existing breadth and sophistication of existing critical approaches and a catalyst to future scholarship.

Developing the psychoanalytical approach through explicit application of the theories of Lacan, Evelyn Jaffe Schreiber investigates the relationship between William Faulkner and Morrison in *Subversive Voices: Eroticizing the Other*. Although this was not published till 2001, I am mentioning it here because along with Patricia McKee's *Producing American Races* (which was published in 1999 and places Henry James alongside Faukner and Morrison), and with Erik Dusseres's *Balancing the Books: Faulkner, Morrison, and the Economies of Slavery* (2003), it marks a culmination of sorts to a series of comparative studies on the two authors. In 1990, David Cowart published the essay "Faulkner and Joyce in Morrison's *Song of Solomon*" (reprinted in the Middleton collection of 1997), which opens with the provocative and not unproblematic assertion that "critical response to 'black' literature tends to overemphasize the adjective and to neglect the claims of the noun it modifies" (95). While Cowart's well-intentioned plea that Morrison "deserves emancipation from her own literary ghetto" is controversial in many ways (not least in the implicitly racialized nature of its metaphor (Cowart 95)), his analysis of thematic and formal affinities of Morrison, Joyce, and Faulkner makes possible the many subsequent positionings of Morrison as a literary figure of global significance whose focus is the black American experience, in other words, as one who transforms the canon by her presence within it.

The pairing of Morrison and Faulkner has proved to be an illuminating project in the hands of many. Some are drawn to this subject by the fact that Morrison wrote her M.A. thesis on Faulkner (and Woolf), and by the compelling affinities and disparities between these two authors' representations of racial identities or in their narrative technique. In 1996 Philip Weinstein published the first monograph on the subject, *What Else but Love?*, which, in a series of pairings of the novels, compares the authors' treatment of the "disaster" of "race relations" in the United States (xxviii). His essay on "fathering" in the two authors is reprinted in the essential multiauthor collection *Unflinching Gaze: Faulkner and Morrison Re-Envisioned* (Kolmerten 1997), in which John Duvall's introductory essay, "The Anxiety of Faulknerian Influence," usefully outlines the issues at stake (Kolmerten 3–16).

A much earlier transracial comparative study is Marilyn Sanders Mobley's *Folk Roots and Mythic Wings in Sarah Orne Jewett and Toni Morrison* (1991), in which the critic defines both authors as "cultural archivists" (7) who, through their attention to purportedly marginal locales, "transform the meaning of universality" (96). Published in the same year, Trudier Harris's *Fiction and Folklore: The Novels of Toni Morrison* constitutes one of the most significant of the many studies of African-American myth and folklore in the oeuvre, arguing that the novels embody "folklore in progress" (11) because "we often can't tell where her imagination leaves off and communal memory begins" (10). In *The Dilemma of "Double-Consciousness"* (1993), meanwhile, Denise Heinze explores the author's engagement with a different kind of mythology – that of national ideology. Organizing her book on a thematic rather than chronological structure, Heinze explores the author's multiple explorations of the "double consciousness" famously defined by W. E. B. Du Bois, as well as the Bakhtinian "double-voicedness" of Morrison herself herself. Philip Page shares many thematic and formal interests with Heinze in his deconstructive reading *Dangerous Freedom* (1995). He demonstrates that the fiction "resonate(s) with the disturbing theme of fusion and fragmentation in poststructuralist theories about American and African-American cultures" (25) and focuses on the paradox of "dangerous freedom" as both a condition experienced by many of the characters and a feature of Morrison's narrative form.

In 1991, Dorothea Drummond Mbalia published the first edition of *Toni Morrison's Developing Class Consciousness*, which she revised for a second edition in 2004. Mbalia enacts a clear developmental reading of Morrison, suggesting that in the novelist's various explorations of "class exploitation" and "racial oppression," "a thread ... runs through and connects novel after novel" (9). Gurleen Grewal, in *Circles of Sorrow, Lines of Struggle* (1998) shares Mbalia's interest in the representation of class conflict but situates Morrison firmly within a broader movement of postcolonialism, making the powerful point that Morrison epitomizes "a minor literature doing the difficult work of decolonization, demystification, and social redress within the dominant language" (18). Morrison also figures as a significant player within the work of key postcolonial theorists of this decade, such as Jonathan White (in *Recasting the World: Writing after Colonialism*, 1993) and Homi Bhabha (in *The Location of Culture*, 1994), and within Paul Gilroy's paradigm-shifting theories in *The Black Atlantic* (1993).

Appearing one year after Grewal's book, Justine Tally's study of *Paradise*, *Toni Morrison's (Hi)stories and Truths* (1999), itself concerned with "the unstable relationship" between "History/history," memory and story (14), is significant for two reasons: it is the first study of a single Morrison novel, and the first book of single-author criticism to be published by a non-U.S. press. Appearing in the Forecaast series (the Forum for the European Contribution to African-American Studies), the book is indicative of the growing international interest in Morrison. Nellie McKay had already included an essay by the major French scholar Geneviève Fabre as well as an account of the German reception by Ann Adam in her 1998 collection. In 1999 the Japanese academic Mori Aoi published *Toni Morrison and Womanist Discourse* – this was the fifth monograph to be published on Morrison by a Japanese scholar in the 1990s.

By the end of this decade, the striking diversity characterizing the critical engagements with Morrisonian fiction was truly apparent. For example, Rosemarie Garland Thomson included in her study the chapter "Morrison's Disabled Women," which was seminal in the emergence of disability studies, *Extraordinary Bodies: Figuring Physical Disability in American Culture and Literature* (1997). A year later Carl Plasa published a totally different kind of book, his invaluable *Toni Morrison, Beloved*. Part of Palgrave Macmillan's Reader's Guide to the Essential Criticism series, this is a wealth of helpfully annotated reviews, source material, and key scholarly essays on that much-discussed text. And the critical divergence about the aesthetics-versus-politics question reached something of a resolution in an important collection edited by Marc C. Conner: *The Aesthetics of Toni Morrison: Speaking the Unspeakable* (2000). The essays here address a range of aesthetic elements in the oeuvre and demonstrate the inseparability of these elements from her political project. It is a book that exemplifies the kind of "both/and" approach, the exegesis of nuance, duality, and ambivalence or conflict within the fiction, that has slowly begun to replace the "either/or" approaches of earlier years.

Since 2000

A second major publication of the year 2000 is John Duvall's study *The Identifying Fictions of Toni Morrison: Modernist Authenticity and Postmodern Blackness*.[8] Duvall positions Morrison as "a historical figure in her own right" and interprets the novels in terms of the formation of her own identity: "One can trace Morrison's personal and professional implications in the things she critiques" (3). His argument that Morrison's "central motivating opposition" is "the tension between identity as a biological essence and identity as a social construction" (9) and that the author combines "a modernist concern with authenticity" with "postmodern fictional practices" is compelling (17). He discusses the relationship between *The Bluest Eye* and Ellison, and between *Song of Solomon* and Faulkner and includes a provocative chapter on rape in *Tar Baby*. His discussion of the relationship between *Sula* and Virginia Woolf sits fascinatingly beside Lisa Williams's book that appeared in the same year: *The Artist as Outsider in the Novels of Toni Morrison and Virginia Woolf* (2000). While you should not miss Barbara Christian's moving second-person address to Morrison on the subject of Woolf (in the Modern Fiction Special Issue of 1993 and reprinted in the Peterson collection of 1997), Williams extends exploration of this relationship by arguing that, despite Woolf's critical blindness on the issue of race, both writers are concerned with "creating an aesthetic that would undermine all forms of domination" (17).

A major poststructuralist study of Morrison's first six novels (and the story "Recitatif") is *Toni Morrison: Playing with Difference* by Lucille Fultz (2003). As its title suggests, this book, which is structured not on each novel in turn but on key "textual moments" in the oeuvre, focuses on the ways in which Morrison simultaneously "sign(s) difference and destabilizes our notions about difference" (19). Fultz engages the concept of "playing" (taken in part from Morrison's own *Playing in the Dark*) to mean both "staging" and "critiquing" (18). A book of similar heft is Rebecca Ferguson's wide-ranging study, *Rewriting Black Identities: Transition and Exchange in the Novels of Toni Morrison* (2007). In this analysis of "the multiplicity of African-American identities" in the successive historical epochs configured by Morrison (11), Ferguson to some extent inherits the focus of John Duvall. Illuminating the novelist's interest in both "transitional eras" and "the interconnected lives of individuals" (18), the critic's incorporation of a wide range of critical approaches and resources – from psychoanalytical theory through questions of narrative and generic form to intertextuality – makes this book a near-comprehensive overview.

Very different in approach from Fultz or Ferguson, in that each is specialized and primarily sociological in its driving investigations, are Angela O' Reilly's *Toni Morrison and Motherhood: A Politics of the Heart* (2004) and Susan Neal Mayberry's *Can't I Love What I Criticize? The Masculine and Morrison* (2007). O'Reilly reads Morrison as a "maternal theorist" (xi) and, studying the novels from *The Bluest Eye* to *Paradise* in the context of scholarship on black motherhood, argues that "Morrison portrays motherhood, in all of its dimensions … as a political enterprise with social consequences" (x). Mayberry, meanwhile, directs our gaze to what she identifies as Morrison's oeuvrewide "review of masculinity" (1). Reading the fiction alongside sociological and psychological theories of black masculinity, this critic argues that, as Morrison envisions them, "not only have black men successfully retained their special vitality in spite of white male resistance; their connections to black women have saved their lives" (1), and that the author's "treatment of her male characters becomes a key to her success in countering the temptations of exclusionary feminism" (4).

As I discuss at more length in Chapter 3, analyses of Morrison's writing within both U.S. and global frameworks have continued in recent years. In *Negative Liberties* (2001), Cyrus Patell identifies the oeuvre as sharing with that of Thomas Pynchon a critique of liberal ideology, in particular that characterizing the Reagan era. In *Tears of Rage* (2008), meanwhile, Shelly Brivic argues for an interpretation of twentieth-century American literature as an ongoing transracial conversation and nominates novels by Faulkner, Richard Wright, Pynchon, and Morrison (he chooses *Beloved*) as his cardinal points. Nancy Peterson's discussion of *The Black Book* and the trilogy in her important study, *Against Amnesia: Women Writers and the Crises of Historical Memory* (2001), considers Morrison alongside Louise Erdrich, Joy Kogawa, and the Holocaust in cultural memory. Adopting a transatlantic approach, meanwhile, Alan Rice builds on Paul Gilroy's work to consider *The Bluest Eye*, *Tar Baby*, and *Beloved* (including the trope of cannibalism) as part of his multigeneric study, *Radical Narratives of the Black Atlantic* (2003).

A critical landmark in the study of the African presences in Morrison's writing is *Toni Morrison and the Idea of Africa*, by La Vinia Delois Jennings (2008). Jennings brings great rigor and learned specificity to her argument that "rich, guiding African traditional cosmologies are at the core of Morrison's fiction" (4). She provides a detailed exegesis of Morrison's engagement with belief systems and structures that center on Kongo's *Yowa* (cosmogram) and Dahomy's Vodun (the Fon word for god) and documents the survival of these structures in the Caribbean's Voudoun, in the United States' Voudou, and in Brazil's Candomblé.[9] Interest in Morrison's allusiveness to the classical tradition continued to develop in this decade as well, keeping pace with the evolution of "black classicism" as a critical field. For example, Patrice Rankine includes a chapter on *Song of Solomon* in his *Ulysses in Black: Ralph Ellison, Classicism and African-American Literature* (2007), and Tracey Walters published *African-American Literature and the Classicist Tradition: Black Women Writers from Wheatley to Morrison* in the same year. While Kathleen Marks's *Beloved and the Apotropaic Imagination* (2002) explores that novel's relationship with ancient Greek religion, the apparent conflict between those critics invested in Morrison's deployment of African traditions, on the one hand, and those invested in her use of European traditions, on the other, reaches something of a resolution in Justine Tally's *Beloved: Origins,* and in my own book, *Toni Morrison and the Classical Tradition* (2013), in which I argue that Morrison enacts a strategic engagement with the interfaces of African and classical tradition.

Further discussion of the novelist's syncretic methods can be found in the critical collection *Toni Morrison and the Bible: Contested Intertextualities,* edited by Shirley A. Stave (2006). As Stave writes, these essays "interrogate and dissect Morrison's use of the Bible, question her theological positioning, and even contest her range of source material" (1). Highlights include Sharon Jessee's chapter on "syncretic spirituality" in the trilogy (129–58) and Jennifer Terry's on Creolization and Candomblé in *Paradise* (192–214). Centered on syncretism of a different kind, meanwhile, a striking recent critical development is the interest in the interactions between African-American and Native American cultures and identities in Morrison's work. Lindsey Claire Smith, for example, addresses this issue in *Indians, Environment and Identity on the Borders of American Literature* (2008). The last decade has also seen a welcome flurry of new comparative approaches, including studies of Morrison and Willa Cather (Danielle Russell, 2006); Morrison and Gabriel Garcia Marquez (Daniel Erickson, 2009); Morrison and James Baldwin (Lovalerie King and Lynn Orilla Scott, 2006); and Morrison, Bessie Head, and Clarice Lispector (Lucia Villares, 2011).

The institutions of canon formation have continued to bestow their laurels on Morrison in recent years. *The Cambridge Companion to Toni Morrison,* edited by Justine Tally, appeared in 2007; many of its useful essays are cited at relevant moments in this *Introduction.* In 2011, the monumental *Cambridge*

History of the American Novel (ed. Leonard Cassuto et al.) devotes its sixty-fourth chapter, by Michael Hill, to "Toni Morrison and the Post–Civil Rights American Novel." Hill places Morrison in the context of her black literary forebears and contemporaries, while announcing unequivocally that she best exemplifies the transition to the richness of African-American literary production since 1970, and that she "stands as barely disputed champ of the African-American novel" (1065). A fitting place to end this survey of the dynamic field that is Morrison criticism is with the special issue of *MELUS* – *Toni Morrison: New Directions* (36.2), edited by Kathryn Nicol and Jennifer Terry – which was published in summer 2011. Its essays are rigorous, politically attuned, diverse in both subject matter and approach; they are a testimony to all that scholarship on Morrison can and should be.

The Status and Reputation of "Toni Morrison"

When considering the reception of Toni Morrison, it is important to be aware of and informed about the phenomenon of "Toni Morrison." By these quotation marks I imply the public figure, the cultural icon whose status and reputation continue to evolve. Following on from the overview of the critical field, I bring this book to a close with an outline both of Morrison's rise to fame and fortune and of the controversy that has sometimes followed that rise.

The story of Morrison's career is one of numerous official recognitions – prizes, appointments, honorary conferrals – but these often have been met with cynical responses and put-downs from some quarters. As the following discussion will show, a pattern has emerged in which nearly every time she wins an award, somebody somewhere announces that the forces of "political correctness" have been at work – in other words, that she only got whichever prize it is because she is a black woman. While in adopting the role of "celebrity radical intellectual" Morrison has not chosen an easy row to hoe, it must in no small part be mainstream culture's incoherence about identity politics, political correctness, and the relationship between art and society that has forced the author into the "damned if you don't, damned if you do" position in which she so often finds herself. As she said to the *New Yorker* journalist Hilton Als in 2003, "I'm already discredited, I'm already politicized, before I get out of the gate" (*GiA* 67).

Morrison first gained widespread public recognition – or the phenomenon of "Toni Morrison" began – in 1977, after the publication of *Song of Solomon*. This novel won the National Book Critics' Circle Award, won an American Academy and Institute of Arts and Letters Award, and was selected as a

Book-of-the-Month Club choice. In 1980 President Jimmy Carter appointed her as a member of the National Council on the Arts, and after the publication of *Tar Baby* in 1981 she was elected to the American Academy and Institute of Arts and Letters, as well as appearing on the front cover of *Newsweek*.[10] It was not until the publication of *Beloved* and the unprecedented levels of both critical acclaim and commercial success that this generated for Morrison, however, that the controversies surrounding her really gained momentum.

While Stanley Crouch's now-notorious review in the *New Republic* of October 1987 described the work as a "blackface holocaust novel" punctuated by "maudlin ideological commercials," as "protest pulp fiction" written by a "literary conjure woman," the British novelist A. S. Byatt, on the other hand, immediately described the book as "a magnificent achievement" and "an American masterpiece."[11] Though most readers sided with Byatt's opinion, the novel did not win the National Book Award at the end of 1987. Enraged by what they described as "oversight and harmful whimsy," forty-eight prominent African-American intellectuals, including Maya Angelou, Amiri Baraka, and Henry Louis Gates Jr., wrote an open letter to the *New York Times Book Review* protesting this fact and attesting to *Beloved*'s worth. Two months later, in March 1988, the novel won the Pulitzer Prize. The timing of events enabled critics to say that the Pulitzer judges were pandering to the pressure of the letter, and the prize could never be seen as a simple recognition of achievement.

Perhaps more troubling were the muttering and the rumbling that surrounded Morrison's winning of the Nobel Prize in literature in 1993. Charles Johnson, a fellow American novelist and fellow African-American novelist, described the decision as "a triumph of political correctness." One wonders how exactly Morrison could be honored, given who she is and the perspective of her fiction, without incurring this criticism. I am also tempted to agree with what she herself said in a 1994 interview: "You know, the term 'political correctness' has become a shorthand for discrediting ideas. ... What I think the political correctness debate is really about is the power to be able to define" (*WMM* 101).

Beloved continues to enjoy more accolades than anything else the author has published. In the spring of 2006, for example, the *New York Times Book Review* asked two hundred prominent writers, critics, and editors, of both sexes and of various ethnicities and nationalities, to answer the question "What is the best work of American fiction published in the last 25 years?" Despite the obviously problematic nature of this question, the clear winner, announced on May 21, was *Beloved*.[12] But the response to the judgment was depressingly predictable. As quoted by the right-wing British broadsheet the *Daily Telegraph*, Roger Kimball, co-editor and publisher of the *New Criterion*, announced that

Morrison "is the perfect *New York Times* poster girl." She is, apparently, "someone whose opinions and skin color immunise her from criticism and whose cliché-riddled, melodramatic prose imparts a hungry urgency to the tired Left-liberal yearnings of the paper's cultural commissars." The *Daily Telegraph* ran the story under the headline "Anger as Literary Giants Lose Out to Slavery Novel," and its reporter, Harry Mount, stated that "the 75-year-old black American edged out giants of modern United States literature such as Philip Roth and John Updike."[13] It is hard to know where to start in unpacking these comments. In 2006, the press of the British establishment still did not consider Morrison to be a "literary giant" or a match for Philip Roth and John Updike, and *Beloved* was referred to as a "slavery novel."

When John Updike died in January 2009, the eulogies in his wake were striking for what they revealed about who, at this time, was considered a "great American novelist." Updike's significance was continually compared to that of Hawthorne, of Mailer, of Roth, of Bellow, and of Auster, but rarely to that of any woman novelist, and never to Toni Morrison. Of course, no two writers could be more different than Updike and she, but what was striking was commentators' failure to invoke Morrison as a figure of equally major and lasting impact. By contrast, only a few months before, Blackwells had published its *Companion to the History of the English Language* (2008), in which Morrison was one of only seven writers chosen for their exemplary deployment of "literary language." The other six were the anonymous author of *Beowulf*, Chaucer, Shakespeare, Austen, Joyce, and Rushdie. To many scholars of her work, it is a given that Morrison holds her head up in such company, yet the reconceptualization of the so-called marginal as central, the full recognition of her significance, is by no means complete.

In her landmark study of American women writers, *A Jury of Her Peers* (2009), Elaine Showalter made the following pronouncement about the author:

> By the end of the century, Morrison was by no means a rural prophet; she had reached that peak of literary veneration at which she became the sibyl and priestess. Her majestic face alone was sufficient adornment for the covers of her books, and took its place alongside Hawthorne, Poe, Twain, Hemingway, and Roth as an American icon. The honor [of the Nobel Prize] accorded to Morrison surely raised the cultural standing of women's writing in general as well as bringing about the canonization of her own work.[14]

This, from a major scholar surveying the entire field, is praise indeed, and it is true that since 2000 Morrison has won far more prizes and awards than can be recorded in the space my *Introduction* permits. Yet in Showalter's assessment, the word "surely" in the last sentence quoted creates a resonance of wishful thinking, an indication of Showalter's awareness of her own role in and responsibility for the correct positioning of Morrison.[15] And one wonders whether the author herself would agree that her job is so completely done. Speaking in Paris in November 2006, she talked about the fact that her books were not studied within many university English Departments in the United States. Of a large state university in Michigan, she said, "I've been on the syllabus in every department you can think of. In Women's Studies, in African-American Studies, in Community Studies, even in the Law Department. But never in the English Literature Department."

The ironies inherent in her reception in Europe, meanwhile, are often greater still. At the University of Oxford, for example, which awarded Morrison an honorary D.Litt. in 2005, she has never to date been recommended as a "special" (or set) author on the English undergraduate syllabus, while Derek Walcott, Philip Roth, and Brian Friel have occupied that position for many years. Arguably, she has always been better received in France than in the United Kingdom, and on 4 November 2010 she was presented with that country's prestigious "Legion d'Honneur." At the award ceremony, the then–culture minister Frédéric Mitterand told her, "In our eyes you embody the best part of America, that which founds its love of liberty on the most intense dreams. The one that allowed a black child born into a poor family in deepest Ohio, in the years of segregation, to have the exceptional destiny of the greatest American woman novelist of her time."[16] Even here, however, Morrison's status is qualified by the description of her gender, as it so often is by one of her race.

The recognition of Morrison as a great writer who is an African-American (and/or American) woman, rather than as a great African-American (and/or American) woman writer; the acknowledgment of Morrison as a global cultural figure whose primary subject is the African-American experience, is a process that is by no means finished. The ongoing work of positioning her correctly, and of comprehending the full implications of her oeuvre, is her readers' responsibility. To borrow from her Nobel Lecture, her project – in all the political, aesthetic, moral, and spiritual transformations it envisions – is in our hands.

Notes

1 Life

1 One useful chronology is *DC* xix–xxiii. Some of the material I use in this chapter is taken from Carmen Gillespie's biographical essay on Morrison in her *Critical Companion to Toni Morrison: A Literary Reference to Her Life and Work* (New York: Facts On File, 2007), 1–15. Henceforth "Gillespie."

2 For discussion of Morrison's names see John Duvall, *The Identifying Fictions of Toni Morrison: Modernist Authenticity and Postmodern Blackness,* 2nd ed. 2000 (New York: Palgrave Macmillan, 2010). Henceforth "Duvall, *Identifying.*"

3 Gillespie, 5.

4 On Morrison's editing and teaching see Cheryl Wall, "Toni Morrison: Editor and Teacher." *The Cambridge Companion to Toni Morrison.* Ed. Justine Tally, 139–50 (Cambridge: Cambridge University Press, 2007).

5 Reprinted in *WMM*, 133–4.

6 See www.tonimorrisonsociety.org. Accessed June 2, 2012.

7 See "Bench of Memory at Slavery's Gateway." *New York Times*, 28 July 2008.

8 Ed. Adrienne Seward and Justine Tally. Private publication, Washington, D.C., 2011.

2 Works

1 In the foreword to *Sula* she reiterates and develops some of this analysis.

2 See La Vinia Jennings, *Toni Morrison and the Idea of Africa* (Cambridge: Cambridge University Press, 2008), 150–3. Henceforth "Jennings."

3 "Etymogically, Sula's name is derived from the designation of a genus of seabird, … an image associated with a dual environment—aquatic and Ariel," writes Lisa Williams. "Sula is both water and bird; fluid and in-flight." *The Artist as Outsider in the Novels of Toni Morrison and Virginia Woolf* (Westport, Conn.: Greenwood Press, 2000), 115.

4 CBS Evening News, 29 October 2008.

5 Gillespie, 413.

6 Kimberly Benston, "Re-weaving the 'Ulysses Scene': Enchantment, Post-Oedipal Identity and the Buried Text of Blackness in *Song of Solomon*." *Comparative*

American Identities: Race, Sex and Nationality in the Modern Text. Ed. Hortense Spillers, 87–109, 97 (New York: Routledge, 1991).

7 See Jennings, 137, 140, 160–3.

8 John Duvall, "Doe Hunting and Masculinity: *Song of Solomon* and *Go Down, Moses.*" *Arizona Quarterly* 47.1 (1991): 95–115.

9 Jennings has explored the names' many echoes of the oral narratives in the Georgia Slave Narrative Collection and the parallels between the game and the "Kongo-and Dahomey-inspired circle dance," the "ring shout" (117).

10 Son reflects on his exile since 1971, and we know he has been on the run for eight years (*TB,* 167; 149).

11 See Jennings, 18.

12 For discussion of the rape scene see Duvall, *Identifying,* 99–117.

13 "Echoes of the Jazz Age." *The Crack-Up.* F. Scott Fitzgerald (New York: New Directions, 1956), 13–33.

14 Marc C. Conner documents the New Testament scholar George MacRae's explanation of "Thunder: Perfect Mind": MacRae describes the text as "a revelation discourse by a female figure," "written throughout in the first person," showing "the extension of the divine into the world." "Modernity and the Homeless: Toni Morrison and the Fictions of Modernism." Keynote Address for the Fifth Biennial Conference of the Toni Morrison Society. Charleston, S.C., 25 July 2008, 10. Reprinted in *Memory and Meaning: Essays in Honor of Toni Morrison.* Ed. Adrienne Lanier Seward and Justine Tally. Private publication, Washington D.C., 2011.

15 Morrison here contradicts her position of 1993, when she tells Angels Carabi that the narrator is the "talking book" rather than a person, and that she thinks of the narrator as "it" (*DC* 94–5).

16 Dorcas in the Bible is raised from the dead by St. Peter (Acts 9: 36–42). For a discussion of the name "Dorcas," and of pastoralism in the novel, see Marc C. Conner, "Wild Women and Graceful Girls: Toni Morrison's *Winter's Tale.*" *Nature, Woman, and the Art of Politics.* Ed. Eduardo A. Velásquez, 341–69 (New York and Oxford: Rowman & Littlefield, 2000).

17 Sharon Jessee, "The Contrapuntal Historiography of Toni Morrison's *Paradise*: Unpacking the Legacies of the Kansas and Oklahoma All-Black Towns." *American Studies* 46.1 (2006): 81–112. Henceforth "Jessee."

18 See Jennifer Terry, "A New World Religion? Creolisation and Candomblé in Toni Morrison's *Paradise.*" *Complexions of Race: The African Atlantic.* Ed. Fritz Gysin and Cynthia S. Hamilton, 61–82 (Münster: Lit Verlag, 2005). Henceforth "Terry."

19 See Terry, 70.

20 Quoted in Jessee, 87.

21 See Terry, 74–5.

22 *Start the Week: Toni Morrison Special.* BBC Radio 4. 8 December 2003.

23 Sottile Theater, Charleston, S.C., July 2008.

24 See Jessica Wells Cantiello, "From Pre-Racial to Post-Racial? Reading and Reviewing *A Mercy* in the Age of Obama." *MELUS* 36.2 (2011): 165–83.

25 See Sandra Kumamoto Stanley, "Maggie in Toni Morrison's 'Recitatif': The Africanist Presence and Disability Studies." *MELUS* 36.2 (2011): 71–88.

26 Abena P. A. Busia, "The Artistic Impulse of Toni Morrison's Shorter Works." *The Cambridge Companion to Toni Morrison,* ed. Justine Tally, 101–11, 102 (Cambridge: Cambridge University Press, 2007). Henceforth "Busia."

27 For a brief outline of the case see http://chnm.gmu.edu/courses/122/hill/hillframe. htm. Accessed 2 September 2012.

28 For an account of the O. J. Simpson case see:http://law2.umkc.edu/faculty/projects/ftrials/Simpson/simpson.htm. Accessed 2 September 2012.

29 The recording of Morrison delivering the lecture at the award ceremony on 7 December 1993 is at www.nobelprize.org/nobel_prizes/literature/laureates/1993/morrison-lecture.html.

30 An important discussion of Morrison's curatorship at the Louvre is Nancy Peterson's forthcoming essay, "Toni Morrison, Théodore Géricault, and Incendiary Art."

3   Contexts

1 These facts are taken from the *The Norton Anthology of African American Literature,* ed. Henry Louis Gates Jr. and Nellie Y. McKay, 2612 (New York: Norton, 1997).

2 Valerie Babb, "*E Pluribus Unum*? The American Origins Narrative in Toni Morrison's *A Mercy." MELUS* 36.2 (2011): 147–64.

3 Tessa Roynon, "The Africanness of Classicism in the Work of Toni Morrison." *African Athena: New Agendas,* ed. Daniel Orrells et al., 381–97 (Oxford: Oxford University Press, 2011).

4 Paul Gilroy, *The Black Atlantic: Modernity and Double Consciousness* (London: Verso, 1993), 4. Henceforth "Gilroy."

5 Paul Gilroy, "Living Memory: An Interview with Toni Morrison." *Small Acts: Thoughts on the Politics of Black Cultures* (London: Serpent's Tail, 1993), 175–82, 179.

6 Duvall, *Identifying,* 16.

7 All the quotations in these seven lines are from Duvall, 17.

4   Reception

1 Jacqueline Weever, "The Inverted World of Toni Morrison's *The Bluest Eye* and *Sula." College Language Association Journal* 22 (1979): 402–14; Barbara Smith, "Toward a Black Feminist Criticism." *Conditions: Two* (1977): 25–44.

2 Cynthia Davis, "Self, Society and Myth in Toni Morrison's Fiction." *Black American Literature Forum* 8.4 (1979): 123–5. Reprinted in Bloom, *Modern Critical Views,* 7–26.

3 Susan Willis, "Eruptions of Funk: Historicizing Toni Morrison." *Black American Literature Forum* 16.1 (1982) 34–42. Reprinted in Gates and Appiah, 308–29.

4 Hortense Spillers, "A Hateful Passion, a Lost Love." *Feminist Studies* 9.2 (1983): 293–323. Reprinted in Gates and Appiah, 210–34.

5 Other significant studies at this time include Marjorie Pryse and Hortense Spillers, eds., *Conjuring: Black Women, Fiction and Literary Tradition* (Bloomington: Indiana University Press, 1985); and Elliott Butler-Evans, *Race, Gender and Desire: Narrative Strategies in the Fiction of Toni Cade Bambara, Toni Morrison and Alice Walker* (Philadelphia: Temple University Press, 1989).

6 Gay Wilentz, "An African-Based Reading of *Sula:*" *Approaches to Teaching the Novels of Toni Morrison*, ed. Nellie McKay and Kathryn Earle, 127–34 (New York: MLA, 1997); and "Civilizations Underneath: African Heritage as Cultural Discourse in Toni Morrison's *Song of Solomon.*" *African American Review* 26 (1992): 61–7.

7 Kimberly Benston, "Re-weaving the 'Ulysses Scene': Enchantment, Post-Oedipal Identity and the Buried Text of Blackness in *Song of Solomon.*" *Comparative American Identities: Race, Sex and Nationality in the Modern Text*. Ed. Hortense Spillers (New York: Routledge, 1991).

8 The book was republished in 2010 with an afterword on *Love* and *A Mercy*: "Toni Morrison's Catholic Letter."

9 A second recent book on this subject is K. Zauditu-Selassie, *African Spiritual Traditions in the Novels of Toni Morrison* (Gainesville: University Press of Florida, 2009).

10 Gillespie, 415.

11 Sanley Crouch. "Aunt Medea." *New Republic* 19 October 1987, 38–43; and A. S. Byatt, "An American Masterpiece." *The Guardian*, 16 October 1987, 13.

12 For an account of the competition and results see A. O. Scott, "In Search of the Best." *New York Times Book Review*, 21 May 2006.

13 Harry Mount, "Anger as Literary Giants Lose Out to Slavery Novel." *Daily Telegraph*, 13 May 2006, 16.

14 Elaine Showalter, *A Jury of Her Peers: American Women Writers from Anne Bradstreet to Annie Proulx* (New York: Knopf, 2009), 494–5.

15 Kathryn Nicol and Jennifer Terry discuss this issue further in their introduction to the *MELUS* special issue, "Toni Morrison: New Directions." *MELUS* 36.2 (2011): 7–12.

16 "Toni Morrison Receives France's Legion of Honour." www.guardian.co.uk/books/2010/nov/05/toni-morrison-legion-of-honour.

Guide to Further Reading

Toni Morrison's Major Works

Novels

The Bluest Eye (1970) New York: Vintage, 1999.
Sula (1973) New York: Vintage, 2005.
Song of Solomon (1977) New York: Vintage, 2005.
Tar Baby (1981) New York: Vintage, 2004.
Beloved (1987) New York: Vintage, 2005.
Jazz (1992) New York: Vintage, 2005.
Paradise (1998) New York: Vintage, 1999.
Love (2003) New York: Vintage, 2005.
A Mercy (2008) New York: Vintage, 2009.
Home New York: Knopf, 2012.

Short Story

"Recitatif." *Confirmation: An Anthology of African American Women.* Ed. Amiri Baraka and Amina Baraka, 243–66. New York: Morrow: 1983.

Libretto

Margaret Garner: An Opera in Two Acts. Rev. ed. New York: Associated Music, 2004.

Nonfiction

"City Limits, Village Values: Concepts of the Neighborhood in Black Fiction." *Literature and the American Urban Experience: Essays on the City and Literature.* Ed. Michael C. Jayne and Ann Chalmers Watts, 35–44. Manchester: Manchester University Press, 1981.

134 *Guide to Further Reading*

"Unspeakable Things Unspoken: The Afro-American Presence in American Literature." *Michigan Quarterly Review* 28 (1989): 1–34.

Playing in the Dark: Whiteness and the Literary Imagination. Cambridge, Mass.: Harvard University Press, 1992.

Lecture and Speech of Acceptance, upon the Award of the Nobel Prize for Literature, 1993. New York: Knopf, 1994.

"Home." *The House That Race Built: Black Americans, U.S. Terrain.* Ed. Wahneema Lubiano, 3–12. New York: Pantheon, 1997.

What Moves at the Margin: Selected Nonfiction. Ed. Carolyn Denard. Jackson: University Press of Mississippi, 2008.

Interviews

Taylor-Guthrie, Danille, ed. *Conversations with Toni Morrison.* Jackson: University Press of Mississippi, 1994.

Als, Hilton. "Ghosts in the Attic." *New Yorker* 27 October 2003: 62–75.

Denard, Carolyn, ed. *Toni Morrison: Conversations.* Jackson: University Press of Mississippi, 2008.

Edited Collections

The Black Book. Ed. Middleton Harris. 1974. New York: Random House, 2009.

Race-ing Justice, En-gendering Power: Essays on Anita Hill, Clarence Thomas and the Construction of Social Reality. New York: Pantheon, 1992.

Birth of a Nation'hood: Gaze, Script, and Spectacle in the O. J. Simpson Case. With Claudia Brodsky Lacour. New York: Pantheon, 1993.

Burn This Book: PEN Writers Speak Out on the Power of the Word. New York: Harper, 2009.

Secondary

Selected one-volume overviews of Morrison's life and work:

Goulimari, Pelagia. *Toni Morrison.* New York: Routledge, 2011.

Matus, Jill. *Toni Morrison.* Manchester: Manchester University Press, 1998.

Smith, Valerie. *Toni Morrison: Writing the Moral Imagination.* Hoboken: Wiley-Blackwell, 2012.

Selected Special Issues of Journals

MELUS 36.2 (2011)

Modern Fiction Studies 39.3/39.4 (1993)

Modern Fiction Studies 52.2 (2006)

Selected Reference Works

Beaulieu, Elizabeth Ann, ed. *Toni Morrison Encylopedia.* Westport, Conn.:
Greenwood, 2003.

Gillespie, Carmen, ed. *Critical Companion to Toni Morrison: A Literary Reference
to Her Life and Work.* New York: Facts On File, 2008.

Selected Criticism

Andrews, William, and Nellie McKay, eds. *Toni Morrison's Beloved: A Casebook.*
New York: Oxford University Press, 1999.

Bloom, Harold, ed. *Modern Critical Views: Toni Morrison.* New York: Chelsea
House, 1990.

Braxton, Joanne, and McLaughlin, Andrée. *Wild Women in the Whirlwind.
Afro-American Culture and the Contemporary Literary Renaissance.*
London: Serpent's Tale, 1990.

Christian, Barbara. *Black Women Novelists: The Development of a Tradition
1892–1976.* Westport, Conn.: Greenwood, 1980.

Conner, Marc C. ed. *The Aesthetics of Toni Morrison: Speaking the Unspeakable.*
Jackson: University Press of Mississippi, 2000.

Cowart, David. "Faulkner and Joyce in Morrison's *Song of Solomon*." Middleton
1990. 95–108.

Duvall, John. *The Identifying Fictions of Toni Morrison: Modernist Authenticity
and Postmodern Blackness.* 2000. 2nd ed. New York: Palgrave
Macmillan, 2010.

Ferguson, Rebecca. *Rewriting Black Identities: Transition and Exchange in the
Novels of Toni Morrison.* New York: Peter Lang, 2007.

Fultz, Lucille. *Toni Morrison: Playing with Difference.* Champaign: University of
Illinois Press, 2003.

Furman, Jan, ed. *Toni Morrison's Song of Solomon: A Casebook.* New York: Oxford
University Press, 2003.

Gates, Henry Louis and K. A. Appiah, eds. *Toni Morrison: Critical Perspectives
Past and Present.* New York: Amistad, 1993.

Grewal, Gurleen. *Circles of Sorrow, Lines of Struggle: The Novels of Toni Morrison.*
Baton Rouge: Louisiana State University Press, 1998.

Harris, Trudier. *Fiction and Folklore: The Novels of Toni Morrison.* Knoxville:
University of Tennessee Press, 1991.

Heinze, Denise. *The Dilemma of "Double Consciousness": Toni Morrison's Novels.*
Athens: University of Georgia Press, 1993.

Hill, Michael. "Toni Morrison and the Post-Civil Rights American Novel."
Cambridge Companion to the American Novel. Ed. Leonard Cassuto,
1064–83. Cambridge: Cambridge University Press, 2011.

Holloway, Karla, and Stephanie Demetrakapoulos. *New Dimensions of
Spirituality: A Biracial and Bicultural Reading of the Novels of Toni
Morrison.* Westport, Conn.: Greenwood, 1987.

Jennings, LaVinia Delois. *Toni Morrison and the Idea of Africa.* Cambridge:
    Cambridge University Press, 2008.
Jones, Bessie, and Audrey Vinson. *The World of Toni Morrison.* Dubuque, Iowa:
    Kendall/Hunt, 1985.
King, Lovalerie, and Lynn Orilla Scott, eds. *James Baldwin and Toni Morrison:
    Comparative Critical and Theoretical Essays.* New York: Palgrave
    Macmillan, 2006.
Kolmerten, Ross et al., ed. *Unflinching Gaze: Faulkner and Morrison
    Re-envisioned.* Jackson: University Press of Mississippi, 1997.
Mayberry, Susan Neal. *Can't I Love What I Criticize? The Masculine and
    Morrison.* Athens: University of Georgia Press, 2007.
Mbalia, Dorothea Drummond. *Toni Morrison's Developing Class Consciousness.*
    Rev. ed. Selinsgrove, PA: Susquehanna University Press, 2004.
McKay, Nellie, ed. *Critical Essays on Toni Morrison.* Boston: GK Hall, 1988.
Middleton, David, ed. *Toni Morrison's Fiction: Contemporary Criticism,* New
    York: Garland, 1997.
Mobley, Marilyn Sanders. *Folk Roots and Mythic Wings in Sarah Orne Jewtt and
    Toni Morrison.* Baton Rouge: Louisiana State University Press, 1991.
Mobley McKenzie, Marilyn. "Spaces for Readers: The Novels of Toni Morrison."
    The Cambridge Companion to the African American Novel. Ed.
    Maryemma Graham, 221–32. Cambridge: Cambridge University Press,
    2004.
O'Reilly, Andrea. *Toni Morrison and Motherhood: A Politics of the Heart.* Albany,
    NY: SUNY Press, 2004.
Otten, Terry. *The Crime of Innocence in the Fiction of Toni Morrison.* Columbia:
    University of Missouri Press, 1989.
Page, Philip. *Dangerous Freedom: Fusion and Fragmentation in Toni Morrison's
    Novels.* Jackson: University Press of Mississippi, 1995.
Peach, Linden. *Toni Morrison: Contemporary Critical Essays.* New York: Palgrave
    Macmillan, 1998.
Peterson, Nancy, ed. *Toni Morrison: Critical and Theoretical Approaches.*
    Baltimore: Johns Hopkins University Press, 1997.
Plasa, Carl, ed. *Toni Morrison, Beloved.* Cambridge: Icon, 2000.
Rigney, Barbara Hill. *The Voices of Toni Morrison.* Columbus: Ohio State
    University Press, 1991.
Roynon, Tessa. *Toni Morrison and the Classical Tradition: Transforming American
    Culture.* Oxford: Oxford University Press, 2013.
Schreiber, Evelyn Jaffe. *Race, Trauma and Home in the Novels of Toni Morrison.*
    Baton Rouge: Louisiana State University Press, 2010.
Smith, Valerie. *New Essays on Song of Solomon.* Cambridge: Cambridge
    University Press, 1995.
Solomon, Barbara. *Critical Essays on Toni Morrison's Beloved.* Farmington Hills,
    Mich.: Cengage Gale, 1998.
Stave, Shirley A., ed. *Toni Morrison and the Bible: Contested Intertextualities.* New
    York: Peter Lang, 2006.

Stave, Shirley A., and Justine Tally, eds. *Toni Morrison's* A Mercy: *Critical Approaches*. Newcastle: Cambridge Scholars Press, 2011.

Tally, Justine, ed. *The Cambridge Companion to Toni Morrison*. Cambridge: Cambridge University Press, 2007.

Paradise Reconsidered: Toni Morrison's (Hi)stories and Truths. Berlin: LIT Verlag, 1999.

Toni Morrison's Beloved: Origins. New York: Routledge, 2009.

Weinstein, Philip. *What Else but Love? The Ordeal of Race in Faulkner and Morrison*. New York: Columbia University Press, 1996.

Williams, Lisa. *The Artist as Outsider in the Novels of Toni Morrison and Virginia Woolf*. Westport, Conn.: Greenwood, 2000.

Online Resources

The Toni Morrison Society online bibliography is accessed via:
www.tonimorrisonsociety.org
On the *Margaret Garner* opera: www.margaretgarner.org

Index

Cambridge Introductions to ...

Authors

Topics